FAST.
SIMPLE.
DELICIOUS.

FAST.
SIMPLE.
DELICIOUS.

60 No-Fuss, No-Fail Comfort Food Recipes
to Amp Up Your Week

TARA IPPOLITO
Creator of Al Dente Diva

PAGE STREET
PUBLISHING CO.

PAGE STREET
PUBLISHING CO.

First published in 2022 by
Page Street Publishing Co.
27 Congress Street, Suite 1511
Salem, MA 01970
www.pagestreetpublishing.com

Distributed by Macmillan, sales in Canada by The Canadian Manda Group.

26 25 24 23 22   1 2 3 4 5

ISBN-13: 978-1-64567-659-1
ISBN-10: 1-64567-659-5

Library of Congress Control Number: 2022938805

Cover and book design by Kylie Alexander for Page Street Publishing Co.
Photography by Christina Branco

Printed and bound in the United States

DEDICATION

To my parents who taught me a true appreciation of food. To my husband who gave me the confidence to pursue it. To my friends who continuously support me. And to all the people that I haven't met who have let me into their homes through cooking. All of you, collectively, drive me every single day to do my best. And to my biggest motivators, Leo and Dominic, I hope these recipes always make you feel like home.

TABLE OF CONTENTS

INTRODUCTION

When did cooking become so complicated? It seems like everywhere I look there are more and more new techniques, spices, seasonings, equipment, gadgets, products and the list goes on. Don't get me wrong, evolution is a good thing. I'm all for finding new ways to serve old favorites. But there comes a point where all of these extra things can become a hindrance rather than a help. No wonder why people are intimidated to try new things or to even start cooking in the first place.

I often get asked, "Don't you ever get tired of cooking all the time?" and the answer is no. I never do. I truly enjoy it. And in writing this book, I think I finally put my finger on why. All of these recipes are easy to make and include familiar ingredients. There are no crazy techniques or new equipment to learn. It's just simply good old-fashioned food. Now that's not to be confused with being boring. No, no, there's nothing boring about any of these recipes. I want to help bring back the idea that great food can be incredibly uncomplicated to make. That's why I originally created my blog, Al Dente Diva, as a place to share easy and delicious recipes without all the fuss. I thought there would be people out there just like me who simply wanted to make great food with ease. As my recipes have grown in popularity, I'm more confident than ever that I was spot on about that.

I get that you're busy because I'm busy, too. I'm a stay-at-home wife and a mother of two very energetic little boys. It gets hectic trying to juggle the responsibilities that just those two roles alone entail, not to mention running a recipe site full-time and trying to maintain any kind of social life. People like us don't have hours to spend preparing meals in the kitchen every night. Cooking doesn't have to be some time-consuming chore we'd rather avoid. The recipes that I've put together in this book will change your mind about what it means to prepare a meal. I know firsthand how busy those weekdays at home can get, when you're tired and have a laundry list of chores to do. I know you can't pour all of your valuable time into making dinner because I can't do that either. Making dinner can be a fun and rewarding experience if you have the right recipes, just like the ones I'm going to share with you in this book. Let's put homemade dinners back on the table with these fast, simple and delicious recipes!

I LOVE THE DOUGH

This chapter title says it all. I really do love the dough, especially when I don't have to make it myself. There's nothing more versatile than cooking with premade dough. The dinner possibilities are limited only by your own imagination. But don't worry, I've already done the thinking for you. Here are my top ten picks for guaranteed crowd-pleasers. They're all easy to make and incredibly delicious. Using premade dough is a great shortcut. These meals will be ready to eat in no time at all. Trust me, once you see how convenient and time-saving it can be, you'll be saying, "I love the dough," too!

SAVORY
SAUSAGE BREAD

Serves 4

Growing up, my mother made this at almost every single family event. It feels like we always had something to celebrate when I was a kid. There was never a lack of food or company. The people I remember. The food not so much. That's because once I heard that Savory Sausage Bread was on the menu, it became my sole focus. Whatever else was being served meant very little to me. It was the only thing I wanted to eat. I've made a meal out of this sausage bread on more than one occasion. Now I serve it to my family the only way I like to eat it since I was a kid. Alone.

2 tbsp (30 ml) olive oil, divided

1 lb (454 g) hot Italian sausage, casing removed

Flour, for dusting

1 lb (454 g) premade pizza dough, at room temperature

1 tbsp (8 g) garlic powder

8 oz (226 g) mozzarella cheese, shredded

Preheat the oven to 350°F (177°C). Line a baking sheet with parchment paper.

In a large skillet, heat 1 tablespoon (15 ml) of olive oil over medium-high heat. Add the sausage to the hot pan. Cook the sausage and, using a wooden spoon, break it into small pieces. Continue cooking the sausage and breaking it into pieces until it's browned and completely cooked through. This should take 6 to 7 minutes total. Once the sausage is done, take the pan off the heat and let it cool slightly.

Lightly dust your working area with flour and roll the pizza dough to about 9 x 13 inches (23 x 33 cm). Do this just like you would roll out a pizza pie. Then distribute the browned sausage evenly over the dough and season it with garlic powder. Sprinkle the shredded mozzarella cheese evenly over the top of the sausage. Be sure to shred it yourself, as it will melt way more easily and be creamier than the pre-shredded stuff in a bag that's usually coated with cellulose. This is a common ingredient in pre-shredded cheese, known for anti-caking and moisture absorption, which prevents it from melting the normal way.

Now jelly roll the dough lengthwise from one end to the other so it looks like a regular loaf of bread. Pinch the ends closed so the filling doesn't come seeping out while it's baking.

Place the sausage bread, seam side down, onto the parchment paper–lined baking sheet. This will help prevent filling leakage, too! Spread the remaining tablespoon (15 ml) of olive oil over the top of the bread and bake it in the oven for 30 minutes, or until the dough is nice and golden. Let it cool for about 5 minutes before slicing it into 1-inch (2.5-cm) pieces and serving warm.

CHICKEN BACON RANCH PIZZA

Serves 4

There's a pizza place by me that has the most incredible thin-crust pies around. My friends and family have been going there for as long as I can remember. A few years ago, they added a chicken bacon ranch pizza to their menu, and to say it became an instant obsession would be an understatement. After many trips to the restaurant, it finally dawned on me: "Hey, I bet I can make this at home." And sure enough, I did! What a deliciously addicting combination of flavors this is, and it's simple to make, too. If you haven't tried this flavor combo on a pizza yet, brace yourself for pure awesomeness.

1 lb (454 g) prepared pizza dough, at room temperature

Flour, for dusting

½ cup (120 ml) ranch dressing

6 slices bacon, cooked and crumbled

1 cup (140 g) shredded rotisserie chicken

½ cup (90 g) diced tomatoes

¼ cup (30 g) diced red onion

Salt and pepper

1 cup (113 g) shredded Cheddar cheese

Preheat the oven to 400°F (204°C).

Roll out the pizza dough on a lightly floured surface and lay it down on a baking sheet. Spread the ranch dressing all over the dough just like you would tomato sauce. Use whatever brand is your favorite. This is going to act as a glue for the toppings.

Now add the bacon crumbles, shredded chicken, tomatoes and red onion evenly over the top of the ranch dressing. Lightly season with salt and pepper.

Next add the cheese, and be sure to grate it off the block yourself. It will melt way more easily and be creamier than the pre-shredded stuff in a bag that's usually coated with cellulose. This is a common ingredient in pre-shredded cheese, known for anti-caking and moisture absorption, which prevents it from melting the normal way. It's worth taking the couple extra minutes to shred the cheese yourself.

Bake the pizza for about 15 minutes, or until the dough is nice and golden and the cheese is melted.

Let it cool for about 3 minutes and slice it into equal-sized pieces for serving.

SAUSAGE AND PEPPERS CALZONE

Serves 4

Calzones are such a fantastic dinner choice. They're super easy to make and can be filled with just about anything. There is something undoubtedly special about a sausage and peppers calzone though. It could be that the meat and vegetables combine perfectly with the cheeses. Now take that perfect combo and wrap it up in golden brown dough. Add some marinara sauce on the side for dunking, and what's not to love? If you've never had one, I highly suggest you give this recipe a try. It will become a new favorite for sure.

2 tbsp (30 ml) olive oil

½ lb (226 g) sweet Italian sausage, casing removed

1 green bell pepper, sliced thin

1 onion, sliced thin

1 tbsp (4 g) Italian seasoning

Salt and pepper, to taste

1 lb (454 g) prepared pizza dough, at room temperature

Flour, for dusting

½ cup (123 g) ricotta cheese

1 tbsp (5 g) dried oregano

1 cup (112 g) shredded mozzarella cheese

1 egg, beaten

Marinara sauce, warmed, for serving (optional)

Preheat the oven to 425°F (218°C). Line a baking sheet with parchment paper.

Add the oil to a large skillet over medium-high heat. Add the sausage, bell pepper and onion. Continue cooking, stirring about every 30 seconds. With your spoon or spatula, break the sausage down into small pieces. Continue cooking until the sausage is browned and cooked all the way through and the vegetables are soft. This should take about 7 minutes.

Season the sausage and vegetables with Italian seasoning, salt and pepper. Then take it off the heat to let it cool a little bit. By the way, you can always use spicy sausage instead of sweet if you want. Even a combination of both would be great. It's completely up to you.

Now cut the dough into four equal pieces. Lightly flour your working surface area and roll each portion of the dough out to about 7-inch (18-cm) circles.

In a small bowl, add the ricotta, oregano and mozzarella cheese. Mix that well to combine all of the ingredients. Now gently stir the sausage, peppers and onions into the ricotta cheese mixture. Then spoon it all over one half of each dough circle until it is evenly distributed.

Pull the dough over the filling and seal each calzone by pressing down on the edges with a fork. You can use your fingers, too, but a fork works fab! Brush the tops with the beaten egg and then carefully put them onto the parchment paper–lined baking sheet.

Bake the calzones for about 15 minutes, or until the dough is nice and golden brown. Let the calzones cool slightly before you serve them. This will help the filing firm up a bit and prevent it from pouring out and making a big mess. I personally love dunking these into a side of warm marinara sauce, but that's totally optional—just strongly recommended by this calzone connoisseur.

ITALIAN
STROMBOLI

Serves 4–6

If you like Italian combos and you like pizza, then Stromboli is kind of like the best of both worlds. It's got all the great flavors of an Italian combo but wrapped in warm pizza dough and served with marinara sauce. This is another staple at the pizza places in North Jersey. We just can't get enough of this stuff. If you've had Stromboli before then you already know why, and if you haven't, then you're about to find out with this super delicious and easy recipe. Try it for yourself to see what makes this a local and personal favorite.

Flour, for dusting

1 lb (454 g) prepared pizza dough

12 slices provolone cheese

12 slices salami

12 slices ham

12 slices pepperoni

1 egg, beaten

1 tsp Italian seasoning

Marinara sauce, warmed, for serving (optional)

Preheat the oven to 400°F (204°C).

Lightly dust some parchment paper with a little bit of flour and roll the dough out into a rectangle shape on top of it.

Leave about ½ inch (1.3 cm) of exposed dough on one of the long ends of the rectangle. This will act as our seal later.

Now, starting on the opposite side from where you're leaving the exposed dough border, cover the rest of the dough with the provolone. Then add the salami, ham and pepperoni in layers. Try to get the pepperoni slices from your deli department if you can. The slices will be about as big as the salami and cover more area than the little rounds that you'd typically see on pizza.

Now jelly roll the Stromboli, ending on that exposed dough border. When you get to the end, push the dough closed with your fingers. Try to seal it as best as you can so the filling stays inside the Stromboli and doesn't seep out. Make sure it's positioned seam side down on the parchment paper to really make sure that filling stays put, brush the top with the egg and sprinkle with Italian seasoning.

Next, take a small knife and cut a few slits in the top for ventilation. About four evenly spaced cuts would be great.

Bake the Stromboli for about 20 minutes, or until the top is nice and golden brown. Let the Stromboli cool and firm up slightly before slicing it into about 1-inch (2.5-cm)-thick pieces. Serve with warm marinara sauce on the side, if you like.

PEPPERONI
ROLLS

Serves 4

I recently learned that pepperoni rolls are originally from West Virginia. I'm not buying it. I just can't see how they didn't originate in Jersey. We love these things here! Every pizza place has pepperoni rolls on display behind the counter when you first walk in, tempting you to buy them with just their presence. This tactic usually works and it works well. I don't think I've ever left a pizza place without one. There's nothing complicated about them, and they're incredibly easy to make. I think the simplicity is what makes them so irresistibly good. Dough, cheese and pepperoni. How could you go wrong?

Flour, for dusting

1 lb (454 g) prepared pizza dough

24 slices pepperoni

½-lb (226-g) block mozzarella cheese, cut into 8 equal pieces

Marinara sauce, warmed, for serving

Preheat the oven to 450°F (232°C). Line a baking sheet with parchment paper.

Dust your working surface area with a little flour. Cut the dough into eight equal parts and roll each piece into a little rectangle. Now add 3 slices of pepperoni and 1 piece of mozzarella into the center of each rectangle. You can use shredded mozzarella if that's all you have. I don't recommend it because it's more difficult to work with, but it's not impossible. So do what you gotta do.

Using the shorter sides first, fold the dough over the filling. Then do the same with the long ends and pinch them closed with your fingers.

Then place them seam side down on the parchment paper–lined baking sheet. Making sure they are seam side down will help keep them from opening during the baking process.

Now make a small slit on top of each one for ventilation. Not too big, about ½ inch (1.3 cm) is perfect.

Bake them for about 10 minutes, or until the dough is golden brown.

Let them cool for a minute or two before serving with a side of warm marinara sauce.

DOUBLE CRUST
CHICKEN POT PIE

Serves 6

Everybody loves chicken pot pie. The filing is so rich and creamy that it complements the flaky crust perfectly. The only problem is that there never seems to be enough of it. The crust-to-filling ratio is way off in most of the chicken pot pies that I've tried. That's why I decided to add a double crust to this recipe. That's right, one chicken pot pie with two delicious crusts. It's finally the perfect amount of filling with the perfect amount of crust. You'll never go back to single-crust chicken pot pie again after you try this easy and doubly delicious version.

3 tbsp (42 g) butter

½ onion, diced

3 tbsp (24 g) flour

1 cup (240 ml) heavy cream

1½ cups (360 ml) chicken broth

Salt and pepper, to taste

½ tsp dried rosemary

½ tsp dried thyme

1 tsp garlic powder

3 cups (420 g) shredded rotisserie chicken

1 (16-oz [454-g]) bag frozen mixed vegetables

2 (9-inch [23-cm]) premade pie crusts

1 egg, beaten

Preheat the oven to 400°F (204°C).

Melt the butter in a large pot over medium-high heat. Then add the onion and cook for 4 minutes, stirring about every 30 seconds, until the onion is soft. Add the flour and cook, again stirring about every 30 seconds, for 2 minutes.

Then add in the cream and chicken broth. Season it with the salt, pepper, rosemary, thyme and garlic powder. Once the liquid starts to form little bubbles and begins to boil, reduce the heat to low. Cook it for about 5 minutes, or until the liquid starts to thicken. Stay by the pot and stir it constantly.

Now turn the heat off completely and add the chicken and frozen veggies. Give everything a big stir until it's evenly combined.

Spray a pie dish with cooking spray and lay one of the pie crusts down on top of it. Pour the chicken pot pie filling onto the crust. Then add the second pie crust to the top and seal it closed with the ends of a fork.

Make a few slits, about four or five, into the top pie crust with a sharp knife. This will release steam while the pot pie cooks so the crust doesn't bubble up and explode.

Brush the top of the crust with the beaten egg and place the pie dish on top of a cookie sheet. I find it's way easier to move the pie out of and into the oven that way. Bake it for about 45 minutes, or until the crust is nice and golden brown. Let it cool for 5 minutes and serve warm.

BEEF AND CHEESE
EMPANADAS

Serves 4

What I'm about to say may shock you, but I didn't have my first empanada until I was in college. Everything is so Italian where I'm from in Jersey that there aren't a ton of Mexican restaurants. They were so good that it made me kind of sad that it took me so long to taste one. I figured the best way to make sure they stayed in my life forever was to learn how to make them myself. I put my own little spin on them of course and took a shortcut with the premade dough so they're way easier to make. This is a great way to make sure that empanadas are always a readily available dinner option for you too.

2 tbsp (30 ml) vegetable oil

½ lb (227 g) ground beef

½ small onion, chopped

3 cloves garlic, minced

1 (1-oz [28-g]) packet taco seasoning

½ cup (120 ml) tomato sauce

Flour, for dusting

1 (1-lb [454-g]) box refrigerated pie crust

½ cup (57 g) shredded Cheddar cheese

½ cup (56 g) shredded Monterey Jack cheese

1 beaten egg and 1 tbsp (15 ml) water, whisked together to make an egg wash

Preheat the oven to 425°F (218°C). Line a baking sheet with parchment paper.

Heat the vegetable oil in a large skillet over medium-high heat. A great way to test if your oil is hot enough to start cooking is with the handle of a wooden spoon. Place the tip of the handle in the oil. If the oil starts to bubble around it, you're in business!

Now once the oil is hot, add the beef, onion and garlic. Break the beef into small pieces using that same wooden spoon and continue cooking for about 5 minutes, or until the beef has cooked all the way through.

Next, add the taco seasoning to the beef and continue cooking according to the directions on the back of the packet. Once the beef is done, add the tomato sauce and simmer that on low heat for about 10 minutes.

On a lightly floured surface, unroll the pie crust. Using a small bowl about 4 inches (10 cm) across, push the rim side down, making four identical circular pie crusts.

Dip your finger in some water and wet the inner rim of each circle. This will help to seal them really well. Now add a little bit of each cheese and about ¾ tablespoon (11 g) of meat filing to one side of the circle. Don't forget to leave a little room so the wet edges are exposed. Fold the other side of the dough over and crimp the edges with a fork.

Place the empanadas on the parchment paper–lined baking sheet and brush the tops with the egg wash. Bake for about 15 minutes, or until they are golden brown. Let them cool for about 2 minutes.

STUFFED
MEATBALL PARMESAN BOMBS

Serves 5 (2 bombs per person)

I'm a big supporter of homemade meatballs. If you happen to have your own recipe or some left over in the fridge, then this would be a great time to use them. If not, no big deal at all. There are some great frozen options out there, and that's a great way to take a shortcut and save some time. I'll leave it up to you to choose your favorite. Either way, once they're covered in mozzarella cheese and baked in a garlicky, buttery crust, no one's going to know or care if they were homemade. All anyone will be talking about is how great they are.

1 (16.3-oz [462-g]) can premade biscuit dough

10 oz (283 g) mozzarella cheese, cut into 10 equal pieces

5 meatballs, cut in half (if you're using frozen, make sure they're thawed)

3 tbsp (42 g) butter

1 tbsp (5 g) grated Parmesan cheese

1 tsp Italian seasoning

½ tsp garlic powder

¼ tsp black pepper

Marinara sauce, warmed, for serving (optional)

Preheat the oven to 375°F (191°C). Line a baking sheet with parchment paper.

Open the dough and take out five biscuits. Split them each in half for ten pieces total. Gently push the dough down with your fingers to make them a little bit wider.

Add 1 piece of mozzarella cheese and 1 meatball half in the center of each biscuit. Stretch the dough out over the mozzarella and meatball and press it together with your fingers to seal it.

Place them seam side down on the parchment paper–lined baking sheet. This will help keep the bombs sealed while they're baking.

Now melt the butter in the microwave and stir in the Parmesan cheese, Italian seasoning, garlic powder and pepper.

Spoon or brush the butter and seasoning over each biscuit. Bake them for 15 to 20 minutes, or until the dough is golden brown. Remember the meatballs are already cooked, so we just want to cook the dough and melt the cheese inside.

Let them cool for about 2 minutes, and I highly suggest serving them with a side of warm marinara sauce for dunking.

GROWN-UP
CHICKEN AND BROCCOLI HOT POCKETS

Serves 4

Don't let the title fool you. These chicken and broccoli hot pockets are loved by people of all ages. I just associate eating them with being a kid. I used to come home from school starving, throw one in the microwave for a minute or two and voila! Dinner was served. As an adult, I still love the idea of a meat-and-cheese-stuffed pastry. The only difference now is that I can make them even better myself. This homemade version may not be as convenient as throwing one in the microwave, but I promise you it will be so worth the extra effort once you taste how much better these are homemade.

1½ cups (170 g) shredded Cheddar cheese

1 cup (71 g) broccoli florets

1 cup (140 g) shredded rotisserie chicken

½ tsp salt

1 tsp black pepper

1 tsp garlic powder

4 tbsp (60 ml) sour cream

Flour, for dusting

1 (1-lb [454-g]) package premade pizza dough

1 egg, beaten

Preheat the oven to 400°F (204°C). Line a baking sheet with parchment paper.

First, shred the Cheddar cheese. Shredding the cheese yourself is a must! It will melt way more easily and be creamier than the pre-shredded stuff in a bag that's usually coated with cellulose. This is a common ingredient in pre-shredded cheese, known for anti-caking and moisture absorption, which prevents it from melting the normal way. While you've got the grater out, shred the broccoli florets, too. This is just a shortcut to get the broccoli into little pieces. I use this little hack all the time and love it.

Now in a large bowl, stir together the chicken, broccoli, cheese, salt, pepper, garlic powder and sour cream.

Sprinkle a little flour on your workspace and lay out the pizza dough. Cut it into four large rectangles.

Distribute the filing evenly among the four pieces of dough onto one side of each rectangle. Then fold the other side over and push down with your fingers to close the seams.

Place them on the parchment paper–lined baking sheet and brush the tops with the beaten egg.

Make three small slits about ½ inch (1.3 cm) long on the top of the dough of each hot pocket. Bake for 15 minutes, or until the crust is golden brown. Let them cool for about 2 minutes and serve warm.

ANYTIME
HAM AND SWISS QUICHE

Serves 6–8

1 tbsp (14 g) butter

½ onion, chopped

6 eggs

1 cup (240 ml) heavy cream

1 tsp salt

1 tsp black pepper

1½ cups (203 g) diced ham

1½ cups (168 g) shredded Swiss cheese

1 (9-inch [23-cm]) premade pie crust

There's no reason to be intimidated by this recipe. The word quiche may sound fancy, but putting this recipe together is not complicated at all. It's really just some beaten eggs with your choice of filling, which makes it a great "clean out your fridge" meal. Put anything in, it all works! I happen to love the ham and Swiss cheese combination the best. As versatile as quiche is, I think my favorite part is how it's served. They can be eaten straight out of the oven or at room temperature. They're great at any time. Both are equally as delicious. So relax and don't stress about this meal being served piping hot. Dinner time is very flexible when you're making quiche.

Preheat the oven to 375°F (191°C).

In a small pan over medium heat, melt the butter and add the onion. Stir every 30 second until it's soft. This will take about 3 minutes. Turn off the burner and let the onion cool slightly.

Now to a large bowl, add the eggs, cream, salt and pepper. Whisk them together until they're well combined.

Next add the ham, Swiss cheese and sautéed onion to the cream and egg mixture. Stir them together until they're combined.

Place the pie crust on top of a baking sheet and pour in the filling. I've accidentally tilted the quiche and spilt some filling transferring it into the oven. The baking sheet keeps it nice and steady during the oven transit. Also, if you do spill, no big deal—it's on the baking sheet instead of the inside of the oven.

Now bake it for about 45 minutes, or until the middle is set. It's easy to test this out, just give the baking sheet a little shake. If the center of the quiche doesn't jiggle and stays firm, it's done.

Let it cool slightly and slice it just like you would a pie. Serve hot, warm or at room temperature.

FOOD GONE FAMOUS

I've been posting recipes to social media for a long time now. I have gained a following across several platforms that I'm proud of and grateful for. But followers don't always share equal views. Some recipes are hits, some are misses but most fall somewhere in between. But every once in a while, lightning strikes and a recipe just takes off. I love when that happens. Watching a video go viral feels like the entire Internet is patting you on the back saying, "We really like what you did here." These are some of the most viral recipes from my social media pages. Not to toot my own horn, but I truly feel they deserve all the attention that they have received. Each one is a hit! I hope you enjoy them as much as so many others have, too.

THE ABSOLUTE BEST **FETTUCCINE ALFREDO**

Serves 6–8

Believe me when I say that after you make this recipe, you will never buy jarred Alfredo sauce again. I mean that. I believe that and I guarantee that I'm right about it. Every single time I post this recipe, the video goes viral. I think that people just can't believe how easy it is to make homemade Alfredo sauce. Oh, and it tastes incredible, too. You just can't beat that kind of combo. I'm so happy that this recipe gets views that are in the millions. The more people that get to enjoy this sauce, the better!

1 lb (454 g) fettuccine

½ cup (114 g/1 stick) unsalted butter

6-8 cloves garlic, minced

1½ cups (360 ml) heavy cream

4 oz (113 g) room temperature cream cheese, cubed

1 cup (100 g) grated Parmesan cheese

¼ tsp salt

1 tsp pepper

1 tsp garlic powder

Dried parsley, for garnish (optional)

Start by boiling salted water in a large pot. You can continue getting the sauce started and drop the pasta into the water once it is boiling. The sauce doesn't take long to make at all and can be left to simmer for a bit. Just cook the fettuccine until al dente.

To start the sauce, melt the butter in a large saucepan over medium heat. Make sure the pan is big enough to add in the pound of fettuccine when it's done.

Now we're going to add the garlic and cook that for about 2 minutes. Keep the heat at medium and give it a stir every 30 seconds or so. We want to infuse the garlic into the butter so the sauce tastes nice and garlicky throughout.

Now add the heavy cream and cream cheese. Whisk that until the cream cheese has melted into the sauce.

Next we're going to stir in the Parmesan cheese. I use the powdered "shaker" Parmesan that comes in a container at the grocery store for two reasons. One, it's way cheaper than the blocks of Parmesan cheese that you have to grate yourself. And two, I was always told the shaker stuff is for cooking and the fresh stuff is just for eating. There really is no difference since it melts into the sauce anyway. So my feeling is if it's cheaper and more convenient, why not use it?

Now it's time to season the Alfredo sauce with the salt, pepper and garlic powder. You can keep this simmering on low heat until the fettuccine is ready. Add a ladle of pasta water to the sauce before you strain the pasta. Adding this salty, starchy goodness will not only thicken and flavor the sauce, but it will also really help the sauce stick to the fettuccine. It's liquid gold!

Once the fettuccine is ready, turn the heat off, drain it and add it to the sauce. Give everything a good toss until the Alfredo sauce is completely coating all the pasta. Garnish with parsley, unless you don't want to disturb the all-white aesthetic. In that case, you can just omit it.

CHEESY **CHICKEN TETRAZZINI**

Serves 6–8

I think this recipe may have initially gone viral for the wrong reasons. There're a lot of questionable-looking ingredients at the start of it. I have a feeling people may have kept watching out of confusion and curiosity. Hey, I don't mind at all. I'm glad it kept their attention long enough to turn their opinion around. Please keep that in mind if you're scratching your head while making this recipe. It's just one of those things that doesn't look too great until it does. You just have to trust me on this one. I'm not exactly sure what happens in the oven that transforms this into one of the most delicious dinners that I've ever had. I've just had to accept that some questions aren't meant to be answered, and that's okay. Try this and I can guarantee you will be pleasantly surprised!

1 rotisserie chicken, shredded

1 (10.5-oz [298-g]) can cream of chicken soup

1 (10.5-oz [298-g]) can cream of mushroom soup

¼ cup (60 ml) sour cream

1 (8-oz [226-g]) block of cream cheese, softened

Salt and pepper, to taste

1 lb (454 g) spaghetti, cooked

1½ cups (168 g) shredded Monterey Jack cheese, divided

1½ cups (170 g) shredded Cheddar cheese, divided

Fresh chopped parsley, for garnish

Preheat the oven to 400°F (204°C).

In a large bowl, add the shredded chicken, chicken soup, cream of mushroom soup, sour cream and cream cheese. Season it with salt and pepper. And add in the cooked spaghetti. Thoroughly mix everything together until it's well combined. Then add 1 cup (112 g) of the Monterey Jack and 1 cup (113 g) of the Cheddar. Gently mix the cheeses in.

Add the mixture to a 9 x 13–inch (23 x 33–cm) baking dish and top it with the remaining ½ cup (56 g) of Monterey Jack and ½ cup (57 g) of Cheddar. Bake it uncovered for 20 minutes, or until the cheese is melted and the sides are bubbling. Add the fresh parsley to the top and let it cool slightly before serving.

SLOW COOKER
BEEF STROGANOFF

Serves 6–8

2 lb (907 g) beef tips

Salt and pepper

1 tbsp (8 g) garlic powder

½ onion, chopped

2 (10.5-oz [298-g]) cans Campbell's® Golden Mushroom Soup

3 tbsp (45 ml) Worcestershire sauce

1 (8-oz [226-g]) package cream cheese, room temperature and cubed

1 lb (454 g) wide egg noodles, cooked

I couldn't even tell you how many beef stroganoff recipes I've tried throughout the years. Most were okay, but I never really found one that I fell in love with. Not until this recipe, at least. I'm not even a huge slow cooker fan but, my goodness, I wouldn't change one thing about this recipe. The sauce is creamy and the beef is so tender. The convenience of the slow cooker can't be ignored either. You can just toss everything in, set it and forget it. This is an amazing dinner choice if you've got a busy day ahead of you. I don't usually push my recipes on people, but I really hope you try this one. It's a personal favorite of mine.

Add the beef tips to the slow cooker and season them with salt, pepper and garlic powder. Add the onion, two cans of golden mushroom soup and Worcestershire sauce. Just be sure you get golden mushroom, not cream of mushroom. They're similar in name but very different in actual taste. The cream of mushroom won't work for this particular recipe.

Set the slow cooker for 7 hours on low. Just set it and forget it. Let it do its thing. When the timer goes off, add the cubed cream cheese and cook for another hour on low. Be sure that the cream cheese is at room temperature so it doesn't clump and blends into the sauce easily.

Give the whole pot a big stir to make sure everything is combined. Serve it warm over the egg noodles.

NO-ROUX
SHELLS AND CHEESE

Serves 6–8

When I first started cooking, I found roux super intimidating. Being a home cook, hearing any culinary term that sounded even remotely complicated turned me off from trying it. I've since come to realize that there's nothing to be scared of. But I've always kept that in mind when creating recipes for people who may be new to cooking. Every single shells and cheese recipe I've come across calls for a roux. I knew there had to be a way to get around that and I was right. This recipe is the creamiest, cheesiest and the most incredibly delicious shells and cheese I've ever had. And guess what? No roux needed. This is by far one of my most popular and highly requested recipes. Everybody loves shells and cheese, but this one in particular is a cut above the rest.

1 lb (454 g) medium pasta shells

¼ cup (57 g/½ stick) unsalted butter, cut into 4 pieces

8 oz (226 g) Velveeta® cheese, cubed

2 cups (480 ml) heavy cream

1 cup (113 g) shredded sharp Cheddar cheese, divided

1 cup (113 g) shredded Cheddar cheese, divided

1 cup (113 g) shredded Muenster cheese, divided

1 cup (112 g) shredded Monterey Jack cheese, divided

¼ tsp salt

1 tsp pepper

1 tsp garlic powder

Dried parsley, for garnish (optional)

Preheat your oven to 350°F (177°C).

Boil the shells in salted water for 2 minutes less than the recommended time on the box. We're going to bake this and don't want the pasta to overcook and turn to mush in the oven.

Next, strain the shells and put them back into the pot. The pot can stay on the same burner, just make sure the heat is off.

Now we're going to add the butter and Velveeta and stir them into the shells. The pasta should still be warm enough to melt the butter. It's okay if the Velveeta stays cubed. It will melt once it's baked in the oven.

Next it's time to add the heavy cream and almost all of the shredded sharp Cheddar, Cheddar, Muenster and Monterey Jack cheese. Make sure to save a little of each to sprinkle on top at the end. I'd say about ¼ cup (57 g) of each is good. It's also really important to shred the cheeses yourself. Don't take a shortcut here and get the pre-shredded stuff in a bag. It will melt way more easily and be creamier if you do it yourself. The bagged stuff is usually coated with cellulose. This is a common ingredient in pre-shredded cheese known for anti-caking and moisture absorption, which prevents it from melting the normal way.

Then add the salt, pepper and garlic powder. Stir everything in the pot together and add it to a 9 x 13-inch (23 x 33-cm) baking dish. Now spread the cheese that we saved earlier evenly over the top and bake uncovered for 30 minutes.

Let it cool slightly before serving. I really like to garnish with a little parsley, too. It gives the dish a nice little pop of color.

SWEET AND SAVORY
TAMALE PIE

Serves 6

It's to be expected that viral videos usually come with a certain number of—hmm, let's call them "critiques." Not this tamale pie recipe. It's like people saw this video and just thought, "Yup, I want some of that!" I can't blame them at all either. This stuff is so good! The beef is savory and the corn bread is a little sweet. The flavors just complement each other so nicely. So many people have tried this recipe and absolutely love it. Make it for yourself so I can add you to the list!

1 (8.5-oz [240-g]) box Jiffy® corn muffin mix

1 egg

¼ cup (60 ml) sour cream

1 (14.8-oz [418-g]) can creamed corn

1 tbsp (15 ml) olive oil

½ red bell pepper, chopped

½ onion, chopped

2 lb (907 g) ground beef

2 (1-oz [28-g]) taco seasoning packets

½ cup (120 ml) red enchilada sauce

1 cup (112 g) shredded Monterey Jack cheese

1 cup (113 g) shredded Cheddar cheese

OPTIONAL TOPPINGS

Jalapeños

Avocado

Sour cream

Cilantro

Sliced black olives

Diced tomatoes

Preheat the oven to 425°F (218°C).

In a large bowl, add the corn muffin mix, egg, sour cream and creamed corn. Stir everything together until it's evenly combined. Add it to either a cast iron skillet or a 9 x 13-inch (23 x 33-cm) baking dish. Smooth the mixture out until it's evenly distributed and bake it for 20 minutes.

Meanwhile, in a large skillet, heat the olive oil over medium-high heat and add the pepper and onion. Cook them for about 4 minutes, stirring every 30 seconds, until the veggies begin to soften. Then add the beef and cook it according to the directions on the back of the taco seasoning packets.

Once the corn bread is finished, using a fork, poke about 10 holes spread out all over the surface. Pour the enchilada sauce on top and cover the sauce with the beef mixture.

Sprinkle the Monterey Jack and Cheddar cheese on top of the beef. Spray a large piece of tinfoil with cooking spray and place it sprayed side down on top of the baking dish. This will prevent the cheese from sticking when it bakes.

Bake the tamale pie for about 20 minutes or until the cheese is melted and the sides are lightly bubbling. Let it cool slightly before serving. Add whatever toppings you'd like!

JERSEY'S FAVORITE PENNE ALLA VODKA

Serves 6–8

Vodka sauce is absolutely incredible! There's something about the vodka that really enhances the flavors of the tomatoes. The cream gives the sauce such a pretty pink color, too. When I first shared my family's vodka sauce recipe on social media, it exploded. People really seemed to love it just as much as we do here in Jersey. If you've never tried it, now is the perfect time to see what all the fuss is about.

2 tbsp (30 ml) olive oil

2 tbsp (28 g) butter, divided

½ onion, diced

6 cloves garlic, minced

2 tbsp (8 g) Italian seasoning, divided

1 tbsp (8 g) garlic powder

1 tsp red pepper flakes (optional)

¼ cup (60 ml) vodka

1 (28-oz [794-g]) can crushed tomatoes

Salt and pepper, to taste

1 cup (240 ml) heavy cream

½ cup (50 g) grated Parmesan cheese

1 lb (454 g) penne

First, heat the olive oil and 1 tablespoon (14 g) of butter in a large saucepan over medium heat. Make sure the pan is large enough to add the penne to later. Once the butter is melted, add the onion. Cook that over medium-high heat, stirring every 30 seconds or so for about 3 minutes, or until the onion is soft. Then add the minced garlic, 1 tablespoon (4 g) of the Italian seasoning, garlic powder and pepper flakes, if you want the sauce to have a little kick. Turn the heat down to medium-low and sauté for about 2 minutes. This is because we want to make sure the garlic doesn't burn. Also, lowering the heat will help the seasonings infuse into the butter and oil. That's going to give your sauce a ton of flavor!

Now we're going to add the vodka. I generally only cook with vodka that I would also drink, so make sure it's of decent quality. Turn the heat up to medium-high and let the vodka gently boil for 2 to 3 minutes. This is going to burn out all the actual alcohol making it safe for kids to eat, too. So don't worry, this is a family-friendly sauce despite its name.

Next, add the crushed tomatoes and season with salt, pepper and the remaining tablespoon (4 g) of the Italian seasoning. Give it a good stir and turn the heat down to low. Let the sauce simmer, uncovered, for 30 minutes. Stir the sauce every 10 minutes or so. After that, add the heavy cream and Parmesan cheese. I always grew up using the powdered Parmesan cheese to cook with. So that's what I always go with. If you choose to use fresh, that's fine. But remember if you need to re-season later that fresh Parmesan tends to be a little saltier than the powdered stuff.

Simmer the sauce uncovered for another 30 minutes. This is a great time to put your salted pot of water on high heat. Drop in the penne once the water is boiling and cook until al dente. Right before you strain the pasta, add a ladle of the pasta water to your vodka sauce.

When the sauce is done, add 1 tablespoon (14 g) of butter. Give that a good stir until the butter is melted. Add the penne to the sauce and toss it all together until the pasta is evenly coated, then serve.

BANG BANG
SHRIMP PASTA

Serves 6–8

I wasn't the least bit surprised when this blew up on social media. I knew when I was making it that something special was happening. I've had bang bang shrimp before and you probably have too. But have you ever had it like this? It's a complete game changer! The sauce should not and absolutely could not be taken for granted here. Adding pasta just seemed like the right thing to do. Sure enough, it was. Not only did I think so, but given this recipe's millions of views, so did the Internet. This one is a winner for sure!

1 lb (454 g) angel hair pasta

1 lb (454 g) baby shrimp

Salt and pepper

1 tsp garlic powder

1 tsp paprika

1 tsp olive oil

1 cup (240 ml) mayonnaise

½ cup (120 ml) sweet chili sauce

½ lime, juiced and zested

1 tsp sriracha

Fresh parsley, for garnish

First, start making the angel hair according to the directions on the back of the package of pasta.

Meanwhile, in a medium-sized bowl, add the baby shrimp and season them with salt, pepper, garlic powder and paprika. Drizzle them with the olive oil and toss everything together until the shrimp are evenly coated.

In a small bowl, stir together the mayonnaise, sweet chili sauce, lime juice, lime zest and sriracha. Set it aside once it's combined.

In a large skillet with a tall lip, add the shrimp over medium-high heat. Stir them constantly until they are cooked all the way through. This should only take 3 to 4 minutes. Once the shrimp just start to curl, they're ready.

Then add the sauce and the drained angel hair pasta to the skillet. Toss everything together until the pasta is evenly coated in the sauce. Serve it warm and garnished with parsley.

SOUR CREAM AND ONION PORK CHOPS

Serves 4

Sour cream and onion is usually associated with a popular potato chip flavor. Maybe you've never thought about it for pork chops before. This recipe is going to completely change your idea of what sour cream and onion means. Instead of chips, juicy bone-in pork chops smothered in sour cream and sliced onions will be all you can think about. This is one of my favorite recipes because it's so unexpected but works so well together. Once you try this, you'll be thinking chops, not chips for sure!

4 bone-in pork chops, 2 lbs (907 g) total

Salt and pepper, divided

1 tbsp garlic powder

Flour, for dusting

¼ cup (60 ml) canola oil

2 large onions, sliced thin

4 cloves garlic, minced

½ cup (120 ml) beef broth

½ cup (120 ml) sour cream

3 tbsp (45 ml) Worcestershire sauce

1 cup (112 g) Swiss cheese, grated

First, season the pork chops with salt, pepper and garlic powder. Then dust them with flour. This just means take a few tablespoons (about 24 g) of flour and lightly coat the pork chops on both sides.

In a large frying pan, heat the oil over medium-high heat. Fry the pork chops on both sides until they're golden brown and cooked all the way through. This should take about 6 minutes total. When they're done, set them aside and keep them warm with a tinfoil tent.

In the same frying pan, add the onions and season them with salt and pepper. Cook the onions over medium-high heat, stirring every minute or so until the onions begin to soften. This will take 7 to 8 minutes. Then add the garlic and cook them together for another minute. Stir every 10 seconds so the garlic doesn't burn.

Now add the beef broth, sour cream and Worcestershire sauce. Whisk the sour cream in until it's nice and smooth. This should only take 1 to 2 minutes. Turn the heat down to low and let the sauce cook for 5 minutes.

Place the pork chops in an oven-safe baking dish and cover them with the sour cream and onion sauce. Top them with the Swiss cheese and broil them until the cheese is melted and bubbling. Keep an eye on this. The broiler can burn the cheese fast, so it only needs a couple of minutes. Serve the pork chops hot!

MOM'S FAMOUS
TORTELLINI SOUP

Serves 6–8

This tortellini soup was famous in the Ippolito house way before the Internet got hold of it. My mother used to make this for my siblings and me all the time. We just loved it and still do, so much so that I make it for my own children now. Mom's original recipe was a little simpler. I've added my own personal touches here and there over the years. But every time I drop that tortellini into the broth, it makes me think of home. Thanks a lot for this one, Mom!

1 tbsp (15 ml) olive oil

1 lb (454 g) sweet Italian sausage, casing removed

½ onion, chopped

4 cloves garlic, minced

1 (28-oz [794-g]) can crushed tomatoes

1 (32-oz [907-ml]) box vegetable stock

Salt and pepper, to taste

1 tsp garlic powder

1 tbsp (4 g) Italian seasoning

½ cup (120 ml) heavy cream

1 lb (454 g) frozen cheese tortellini

¼ cup (25 g) grated Parmesan cheese

In a large pot, heat the olive oil over medium-high heat. Add the sausage and onion. With a wooden spoon, break up the sausage into little pieces as it browns. Keep doing this until it's all broken up and the sausage is cooked all the way through. Then add the garlic and sauté that for another minute. Stir about every 10 seconds so the garlic doesn't burn.

Now add the crushed tomatoes and vegetable stock. Stir those together and season with salt, pepper, garlic powder and Italian seasoning. Let it all cook for about 5 minutes. Give it a stir every minute or so.

Next add the heavy cream and frozen tortellini. Stir the pasta into the sauce and let it cook for about 6 minutes. You'll know the tortellini is done once it plumps up a bit on the surface.

Stir in the Parmesan cheese and serve warm.

CREAMY
TOMATO AND SPINACH BOW TIES

Serves 6–8

I usually start this recipe video off by saying, "This is the best pasta with the least amount of effort." Now doesn't that sound intriguing? It should because it's true. This pasta takes barely any time at all to make and is loaded with incredible flavors. This is a great example of good food not having to take a ton of work to put together. People seem to really appreciate this one and I'm so glad. It makes me happy that it became so popular because it's a personal favorite of mine too.

1 lb (454 g) bow tie pasta

1 tbsp (15 ml) olive oil

½ onion, chopped

4 cloves garlic, chopped

1 (14.5-oz [411-g]) can diced tomatoes, with juices

⅓ cup (80 ml) heavy cream

Salt and pepper, to taste

1 tsp Italian seasoning

1 tsp garlic powder

2 cups (60 g) fresh baby spinach

¼ cup (25 g) grated Parmesan cheese, plus more for topping

First, start boiling the bow ties according to the directions on the back of the pasta package. If the pasta is done before the sauce, just be sure to keep a ladle of that pasta water before draining. We're going to need it for the sauce.

In a medium-sized pot, heat the olive oil over medium-high heat. Add the onion and cook for about 4 minutes, stirring every 30 seconds, or until the onion begins to soften. Then add the garlic and cook that for another minute. Stir that about halfway through so the garlic doesn't burn.

Now add the diced tomatoes and heavy cream. Season it with salt, pepper, Italian seasoning and garlic powder. Stir it until it's evenly combined. Turn down the heat to low and let it simmer for about 5 minutes.

Add the ladle of pasta water and the drained bow ties to the sauce. Then, in batches, add the spinach to the pasta and sauce. Stir it in until it's all wilted down.

Next add the cheese and give it one last stir to combine it all. I recommend serving it with a little more Parmesan cheese on top!

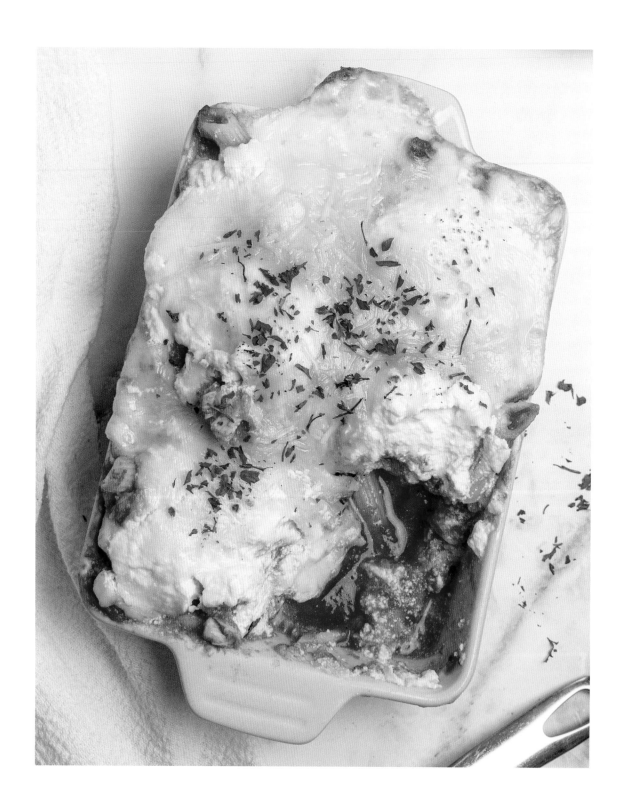

RECIPE REMIXES

You may be asking yourself, what exactly is a recipe remix? Great question, and I'm here with an answer. This is my own way of describing a dish that you're probably already familiar with but is served in a brand-new way. It's a place to really have some fun in the kitchen by getting creative. We're going to reinvent old favorites, combine foods from different cultures and even pair unlikely ingredients. And guess what? It all works! I know because I already did all of the culinary experimenting for you. These recipe remixes are also examples of how food can be a great conversation starter, too. So serve something a little different at dinner next time. Who knows? It may just spark an interesting conversation.

BUFFALO
CHICKEN PASTA

Serves 6

This may just be the best recipe remix of all time. Serious question: have you ever tried to stop eating buffalo chicken dip? It's next to impossible. I've never seen that stuff survive at a party for longer than 15 minutes. Now imagine it over yet another almost-impossible-to-stop-eating food: pasta. This dish is beyond delicious. Just be aware that once you pick up your fork, it may be very hard to put back down.

2½ cups (350 g) shredded rotisserie chicken

½ cup (120 ml) ranch or blue cheese dressing

Salt and pepper, divided, to taste

2 tbsp (28 g) butter

¼ cup (25 g) chopped celery

1 (14.5-oz [411-g]) can diced tomatoes, with juices

4 cups (960 ml) chicken broth

1 lb (454 g) penne

½ cup (120 ml) buffalo sauce

6 oz (170 g) cream cheese, softened at room temperature

1½ cups (168 g) shredded Monterey Jack cheese

1½ cups (170 g) shredded Cheddar cheese

1 tbsp (8 g) garlic powder

In a medium-sized bowl, mix together the shredded chicken and ranch dressing. You can use blue cheese if you prefer. I actually do! But most people prefer ranch, so when I'm cooking for a group, I usually just play it safe with the ranch. Lightly season the chicken mixture with salt and pepper, stir it all together and set it aside.

Now melt the butter in a large pot over medium-low heat. Add the celery and sauté, stirring every 30 seconds or so until it's just soft. You want to be sure to leave a tiny bit of crunch to it still. This will take about 5 minutes.

Add the diced tomatoes and chicken broth to the pot. Season with a little bit of pepper here. No salt is needed because the broth is salty enough. Bring it to a boil over high heat.

Once it's at a boil, add in the penne. Cover it and let it boil for about 10 minutes. Boiling the pasta in the tomatoes and chicken broth is going to give it a ton of great flavor.

Lower the heat to a simmer and add the buffalo sauce, cream cheese and shredded Monterey Jack and Cheddar cheeses. Make sure the cream cheese is at room temperature before you do this so it blends together with ease. Also, shredding the Cheddar and Monterey Jack cheese yourself is a must. It will melt way more easily and be creamier than the pre-shredded stuff in a bag that's usually coated with cellulose. This is a common ingredient in pre-shredded cheese known for anti-caking and moisture absorption, which prevents it from melting the normal way. Stir everything together until it's well combined.

Now gently stir in the shredded chicken and garlic powder. Taste it and add more salt and pepper if you think it needs it. Serve warm.

CHICKEN
ENCHILADA CASSEROLE

Serves 8–10

There's so much to enjoy about this recipe. For starters, who doesn't just love Mexican food? Chicken enchiladas are a favorite around my house. As much as my family loves them, sometimes the time it will take to make them stops me from actually doing it. That's the beauty of this recipe. It's all the amazing flavors of chicken enchiladas with the convenience of putting together a casserole. Such little time and effort with maximum deliciousness. This recipe is the perfect win-win.

1 tbsp (15 ml) olive oil

1 small onion, diced

1 red bell pepper, diced

2 jalapeños, diced (optional)

1 (15-oz [425-g]) can black beans, rinsed and drained

1 (15-oz [425-g]) can pinto beans, rinsed and drained

1 (8-oz [226-g]) can of corn, drained

3 cups (420 g) shredded rotisserie chicken

Salt and pepper, to taste

½ tsp cumin

½ tsp chili powder

½ tsp cayenne pepper

3 cups (720 ml) red enchilada sauce, divided

12 corn tortillas, divided

1½ cups (168 g) shredded Monterey Jack cheese, divided

1½ cups (170 g) shredded Cheddar cheese, divided

OPTIONAL TOPPINGS

Sour cream

Black olives

Cilantro

Parsley

Diced tomatoes

Preheat the oven to 375°F (191°C).

In a large skillet, add the oil over medium heat. Once the oil is hot, add the onion and bell pepper. Cook the vegetables for about 5 minutes, or until they're soft. Make sure to give them a stir every 30 seconds or so. Next add the jalapeños if you're using them, the black beans, the pinto beans, the corn and the chicken. Season with salt, pepper, cumin, chili powder and cayenne pepper.

Turn the heat off and then add 2 cups (480 ml) of enchilada sauce and stir everything together until it's evenly combined. Now take about ½ cup (120 ml) of enchilada sauce and spread it on the bottom of a 9 x 13–inch (23 x 33–cm) baking dish.

Time to layer! Take 6 tortillas and place them on the bottom of the baking dish. Try to cover as much of the bottom of the baking dish as possible. Overlapping is fine. Also keep in mind that the tortillas can be cut, so feel free to rip them into pieces to make them fit the baking dish.

Then add about half of the chicken mixture and spread it out evenly over the tortillas. Sprinkle half of each of the Monterey Jack and Cheddar cheeses on top evenly also. Repeat with a final layer of tortillas and then the remaining chicken mixture. This time we're going to pour the remaining enchilada sauce on top of the chicken before adding the rest of the shredded cheeses.

Spray some tinfoil with some cooking spray and place it sprayed side down to cover the top of the baking dish. Doing this will make sure that none of cheese sticks to the top when it's baking in the oven. This is a great tip to use when cooking with tinfoil. It's saved me from wasting a lot of cheese that would normally get stuck to the top and thrown away.

Now bake it for 30 minutes, or until the sides are bubbly and the top is golden brown. Let it cool off and rest for 5 to 10 minutes before adding your desired toppings and slicing into it. I like some dollops of sour cream, black olives, cilantro or parsley and diced tomato, but you choose whatever you like.

MEXICAN LASAGNA

Serves 6–8

A beautiful thing happens when the incredible flavors of Mexico combine with Italian ingenuity. The Mexican lasagna is born, and let me tell you, it's just as incredible as it sounds. We're going to use large tortillas as lasagna sheets, taco-seasoned beef instead of traditional meat sauce and replace mozzarella with a shredded blend of Mexican cheeses. *Que bueno*, am I right? It all comes together so perfectly that you may start to wonder why you've never eaten it this way before. But let's not look at the past and instead focus on all the opportunities for this incredibly easy Mexican Lasagna to grace your dinner table in the future.

1½ lb (680 g) ground beef

2 (1-oz [28-g]) taco seasoning packets

2 tbsp (30 ml) olive oil

1 medium onion, chopped

1 red bell pepper, chopped

4 cloves garlic, minced

1 (28-oz [794-g]) can crushed tomatoes

Salt and pepper

½ cup (120 ml) canola oil

12 corn tortillas

1 (15-oz [425-g]) can black beans, drained, divided

2 cups (224 g) shredded Monterey Jack cheese, divided

2 cups (226 g) shredded Cheddar cheese, divided

OPTIONAL TOPPINGS

Sour cream

Salsa

Guacamole

Preheat the oven to 350°F (177°C).

First, make the ground beef according to the directions on the taco seasoning packet. I put two packets in the ingredients because we're using a little over a pound of beef. You don't need to use the whole second packet unless you want the extra seasoning; it's completely up to you.

In a large skillet, heat the olive oil over medium-high heat. Add the onion and bell pepper and cook them for about 5 minutes. Give it a good stir every 30 seconds or so. Then add the garlic and cook for another minute.

Reduce the heat to medium-low and add the crushed tomatoes. Lightly season with salt and pepper and continue cooking for about 15 minutes. If the tomatoes are splattering out of your pan, just reduce the heat a little. Make sure to stir it every couple of minutes.

In another skillet, heat the canola oil over medium high heat. Once the oil is hot, fry the tortillas one at a time until they are slightly browned on both sides. This will only take about 1 to 2 minutes for each one. Drain them on paper towels or a wire rack until you have all of them nice and crispy.

Lightly spray a 9 x 13–inch (23 x 33–cm) baking dish with cooking spray and place 4 tortillas down. They will overlap a little. That's okay! Now it's time to assemble this lasagna-style. Evenly spread half of the beans over the top of the tortillas. Then add half of the meat mixture. Next add about one-third of the cheeses and half of the tomato sauce. Top that with 4 more tortillas and repeat that layering process until you get to the end and there are 4 tortillas on top. Sprinkle with the remaining cheese and bake uncovered for about 40 minutes. Remember the beef is already cooked, so we just want to melt the cheese and bake everything together.

Now this is important: Let the Mexican Lasagna sit for about 10 minutes before serving. If you try to cut into it before then, it will not hold its shape. Everything will just pour out in one big gloopy mess. Serve this warm with sour cream, salsa, guacamole or whatever you're in the mood for!

SHEPHERD'S PIE
BAKED POTATOES

Serves 4

I think it's fair to assume that most of us have had Shepherd's pie at some point in our lives. But I bet you've never had it like this before. There's a small tweak; nothing too drastic but different nonetheless. Instead of eating the mixture of ground beef and veggies under a bed of mashed potatoes, we're going to serve it on top of a nice big buttery baked potato. This is a faster way to make it, too. The dish still keeps all of its original great flavor but is served in a new fun way. Such a perfect dinner choice for a cold winter night when you're looking for a hearty stick-to-your-ribs meal.

4 large russet potatoes

1 tbsp (15 ml) vegetable oil

1 lb (454 g) ground beef or meat of choice

1 medium onion, chopped

4 cloves garlic, minced

Salt and pepper, divided

1 (6-oz [170-g]) can tomato paste

¼ cup (60 ml) Worcestershire sauce

1½ cups (360 ml) beef broth

2 cups (268 g) frozen mixed vegetables, thawed (there can be others included, but get a bag that's got peas and carrots in it)

Butter (optional)

1 cup (113 g) shredded Cheddar cheese

Preheat the oven to 400°F (204°C). Line a baking sheet with parchment paper.

Fork the potatoes in several spots all over the surface and place them in a microwaveable bowl. Microwave them for about 10 minutes or until you can easily pierce them with a knife. You can bake them in the oven too if you'd like, but that can take up to an hour, and who's got that kinda time? The microwave is a great shortcut.

In the meantime, heat the oil over medium-high heat in a large skillet. Then add the beef, onion, garlic, salt and pepper. Break the beef into small pieces using a wooden spoon while cooking. It should take about 5 minutes until the meat is cooked all the way through.

Now add the tomato paste and cook that into the beef mixture for about 2 minutes, stirring once every 30 seconds. Then add the Worcestershire sauce and beef broth. Cook together for about 5 minutes, stirring every minute or so.

Re-season with salt and pepper. Just keep in mind that the beef broth adds a lot of salt already. Add the frozen veggies and stir them into the broth mixture for about 2 minutes, or until the vegetables have thawed.

Next, cut the potatoes in half lengthwise and add them to the parchment paper–lined baking sheet. Season them with salt and pepper. You can even add a little butter here if you'd like, too. Evenly spoon the filling over each potato and top it with the cheese.

Bake them for 8 to 10 minutes, or until the cheese has melted on top. Serve them warm.

CHEESESTEAK
SLOPPY JOES

Serves 6

Cheesesteak Sloppy Joes are the food hybrid no one knew they needed until now. My mouth is watering just thinking about them. Imagine seasoned ground beef mixed with melted cheese in between a toasted brioche bun. It doesn't get much better than that, folks. They're incredibly quick and easy to make because there aren't a ton of ingredients. Sometimes less is more, and that's exactly what's going on in this case. Try these once and I bet they claim a permanent spot on your rotating dinner menu.

1 lb (454 g) ground beef

2 tbsp (28 g) butter

½ onion, chopped

½ green bell pepper, chopped

1 tbsp (15 ml) yellow mustard

2 tbsp (30 ml) ketchup

2 tbsp (30 ml) Worcestershire sauce

Salt and pepper, to taste

6 oz (170 g) Velveeta cheese, cubed

6 toasted brioche buns

Add the ground beef to a hot skillet over medium-high heat. Stir the ground beef and break it up into small pieces as you cook it. When it's browned and cooked all the way through, which should take 5 to 7 minutes, remove the beef from the pan and set it aside in a bowl.

Now, in the same skillet over medium-high heat, add the butter. Once it's melted, add the onion and bell pepper. Continue cooking, stirring once every 30 seconds or so until the veggies are soft. This should only take about 5 minutes total. Peppers and onions in a cheesesteak can be a super controversial subject depending on where you're from. I think they're a must! But if you're someone who thinks they absolutely do not belong in a cheesesteak, then I can totally respect that. Just omit them—no big deal at all.

Reduce the heat to low and add the beef back into the pan along with the mustard, ketchup, Worcestershire sauce, salt and pepper. Give it a good stir until everything is well combined.

Now time for another controversial ingredient, the Velveeta. People tend to choose provolone cheese when doing cheesesteaks because that's what they use in Philly. I gotta be honest, I don't care for it too much. The Velveeta tastes more like the cheesesteaks we get on the Jersey shore boardwalk, and I just love that. It also helps make the sloppy joes just a little bit less sloppy by binding everything together. So if you're like me and prefer this way, add the cubed Velveeta now and gently stir it in until it's all melted and well incorporated. If you prefer provolone, just skip this step and add the slices after you add your meat to the bun.

Spoon the beef mixture on top of the toasted brioche buns. Brioche buns are soft, airy and delicious! Toasting them will help create a little barrier so the beef mixture doesn't get the bread too soggy. Serve warm.

SOUTHWESTERN EGG ROLLS WITH AVOCADO RANCH DIPPING SAUCE

Egg rolls might not immediately come to mind when you think of Southwestern food, but maybe they should. Or should I say, maybe they will now after trying these! There is something so special about this combination that makes you feel like they've belonged together the entire time. It's like a flavor bomb in every single bite. Don't worry if you've never worked with egg roll wrappers before. There's nothing to it!

Serves 8 (2 egg rolls each)

2 tbsp (18 g) taco seasoning, divided

1 cup (140 g) shredded chicken

1 tbsp (15 ml) vegetable oil, plus more for frying

½ red bell pepper, minced

½ onion, minced

½ cup (68 g) frozen corn

½ cup (86 g) cooked black beans, rinsed and drained

¼ cup (39 g) frozen spinach, thawed and drained

1 cup (112 g) shredded Monterey Jack cheese

16 egg roll wrappers

AVOCADO RANCH SAUCE

½ avocado, mashed

1 (1-oz [28-g]) package dry ranch dressing mix

½ cup (120 ml) milk

½ cup (120 ml) mayonnaise

First, in a large bowl, add 1 tablespoon (9 g) of the taco seasoning to the shredded chicken. Mix it together and set it aside for now.

In a large skillet, heat a tablespoon (15 ml) of vegetable oil over medium-high heat. Add the pepper and onion and cook for 2 minutes. Stir every 30 seconds or so. Then add the corn, beans, spinach and the remaining tablespoon (9 g) of taco seasoning. Cook for another 3 minutes, stirring every 30 seconds. Turn the heat off and let the mixture cool slightly.

Now add the cheese and vegetable mixture to the chicken. Stir everything together until it's well combined. Divide the filling evenly into the center of each egg roll wrapper. Follow the sealing directions on the egg roll wrapper package until they're all sealed.

In a large skillet with a tall-brimmed lip, heat some of the remaining vegetable oil over medium-high heat. Put just enough vegetable oil into the skillet so that it covers the bottom of the pan by 1½ inches (4 cm). When the oil hits 350°F (177°C), it's ready to use. If you don't have a kitchen thermometer to check the temperature, I have a trick that works every time. Take a wooden spoon and place it into the oil, handle side down. If bubbles form around the spoon, that means the oil is hot enough and ready to go!

Carefully place the egg rolls down into the hot oil and fry them on all sides until they are golden brown. This should take 5 to 7 minutes total. When they're done, place them onto a wire rack to drain the extra oil and cool.

While those are cooling, make the avocado ranch dipping sauce. Add all of the ingredients to a small bowl and whisk them together. Slice the egg rolls down the center in a diagonal crosscut and serve with the avocado ranch dipping sauce.

FRENCH ONION
SALISBURY STEAKS

Serves 5

In general, I don't think Salisbury steaks get nearly enough attention. They're often associated with bad TV dinners or cafeteria food. That couldn't be farther from the truth. They're delicious, easy to put together and budget friendly. The only thing that could make Salisbury steaks more appealing would be to remix them with French onion soup. Add some caramelized onions and a little melted cheese and we've got a winner! This is just the upgrade Salisbury steaks need to finally get the credit that they deserve.

1½ lb (680 g) ground beef

1 egg

4 tbsp (60 ml) Worcestershire sauce, divided

¾ cup (81 g) Italian seasoned breadcrumbs

2 tbsp (16 g) garlic powder

Salt and pepper

4 tbsp (57 g) butter

2 large onions, thinly sliced

¼ cup (31 g) flour

2 cups (480 ml) beef broth

10 slices Swiss cheese

In a large bowl, add the ground beef, egg, 2 tablespoons (30 ml) of the Worcestershire sauce, breadcrumbs, garlic powder, salt and pepper. Mix everything with your hands just until it's evenly combined. Be sure not to overmix the meat. Overworking the meat can lead to a super dense Salisbury steak, and we want to keep them nice and light.

Next, divide the meat into five even portions and roll them into balls. Gently press down with your hands, making little meat-looking hockey pucks.

In a large skillet, melt the butter over medium-high heat. Add the beef patties and brown them for about 4 minutes on each side. Place them on a plate and cover them with tinfoil to keep them warm when they are done.

Now it's time for the sauce! Reduce the heat to medium and add the onions. Give them a good stir every 30 seconds or so until they're soft. This should take about 5 minutes. Sprinkle the flour on top of the onions and continue cooking and stirring for 1 to 2 minutes. We want to be sure to cook out all that bitter taste of the flour.

Next, slowly add in the beef broth and the remaining 2 tablespoons (30 ml) of Worcestershire sauce. Stir the onions into the broth and make sure to scrape any browned bits that have stuck to the bottom of the pan. This is going to release so much flavor! Turn the heat up until the broth just starts to bubble, then reduce the heat to a low simmer.

Add the beef patties back into the pan, cover it and let them simmer in the sauce for about 5 minutes. Then top each one with two slices of Swiss cheese and place the lid back on for about 2 more minutes. You know it's ready to serve when the cheese is melted and the sauce has thickened. Serve warm.

CHICKEN PARMESAN
BAKED ZITI

Serves 6

The idea for this recipe was so simple. It came to me one day after serving baked ziti and chicken Parmesan at Sunday dinner for the thousandth time. I noticed that I kept forking a few pieces of baked ziti with every bite of chicken parm. I wondered how long I'd been unconsciously eating it this way. All I was sure of was that I couldn't remember not doing it. They just complemented each other so well. It was then that I decided to create this recipe using shredded chicken as a time-saver, and it was a pure match made in heaven. Yes, these two dishes are incredible on their own, but together is where they belong.

1 lb (454 g) penne pasta

2 cups (280 g) shredded rotisserie chicken

3 cups (720 ml) tomato sauce, jarred or homemade

1 tsp garlic powder

2½ cups (280 g) shredded mozzarella cheese, divided

¼ cup (62 g) ricotta cheese

½ cup (50 g) Parmesan cheese, grated

Fresh chopped parsley, for garnish

Preheat the oven to 375°F (191°C).

First cook the pasta according to the al dente instruction on the back of the package. After it's drained, add it back to the pot you just used to boil it in.

Add the chicken, tomato sauce and garlic powder to the pot. Stir that all together until everything is evenly combined. You've probably noticed we didn't bread the chicken like traditional chicken Parmesan. Don't worry at all, I promise you won't even be able to tell. The cheese and sauce smother it so that there's no need. Plus, doing it this way is a huge time-saver.

Then add 1½ cups (168 g) of the mozzarella cheese. Make sure to shred it yourself or it won't melt as well. Gently stir it into the pasta.

Pour half of the pasta into a 9 x 13-inch (23 x 33-cm) baking dish. Now take a tablespoon and place dollops of the ricotta cheese on top of the pasta. Try your best to evenly distribute them with some space in between.

Now pour the rest of the pasta into the baking dish. Top it with the Parmesan and remaining cup (112 g) of the mozzarella cheese.

Bake it for about 30 minutes, or until the cheese on top is melted and the edges are lightly bubbling. When you remove it from the oven, let it cool slightly and add the freshly chopped parsley for garnish.

EGGPLANT MEATBALLS AND SPICY MARINARA SAUCE

Serves 6

The title of this recipe is a little misleading. There isn't any actual meat in these meatballs. I hope that doesn't put you off to the idea. I first had them at a local restaurant when I ordered them on a whim not knowing what to expect. They came as an appetizer plate of four and were meant to be shared. I had one taste and decided I wasn't going to share them with anybody. They were so different and delicious that I couldn't get enough. Of course, I had to experiment at home until I figured out exactly how to make them. So yeah, there isn't any meat in this recipe, but trust me, you're not even going to miss it.

FOR THE TOMATO SAUCE

1 tbsp (15 ml) olive oil

½ small onion, chopped

4 cloves garlic, chopped

1 tbsp (5 g) crushed red pepper flakes

1 (28-oz [794-g]) can crushed tomatoes

Salt and pepper, to taste

2 tbsp (8 g) Italian seasoning

1 tsp garlic powder

FOR THE EGGPLANT MEATBALLS

2 lb (907 g) eggplant, peeled and cut into cubes

Salt and pepper, to taste

1 tbsp (8 g) garlic powder

2 cups (216 g) Italian seasoned breadcrumbs

1 large egg

¼ cup (31 g) flour

¼ cup (25 g) shredded Parmesan cheese

Preheat the oven to 350°F (177°C). Line a baking sheet with parchment paper.

Start by making the tomato sauce so it can simmer while the meatballs cook. Heat the olive oil over medium-high heat and add the onion and garlic. Stir them about every 30 seconds. After 2 minutes, add the crushed red pepper flakes and continue to cook, still stirring every 30 seconds, for another 3 minutes. Now add the crushed tomatoes, salt, pepper, Italian seasoning and garlic powder. Let this simmer on the lowest heat setting while we make the eggplant meatballs.

In a large pot, boil water and add the eggplant. Cook it until the cubes are fork tender, about 10 minutes. Drain the eggplant cubes when they're done and gently press them into a dish towel. Try to remove as much moisture as you can from them.

Add the eggplant to a large bowl. Then add the salt, pepper, garlic powder, breadcrumbs, egg, flour and Parmesan cheese.

Roll the eggplant into medium-sized meatballs. The consistency can be a little wet to work with. Just do your best; they don't have to look perfect. Place them onto the parchment paper–lined baking sheet and bake them for 25 minutes.

The eggplant meatballs are delicate, so gently toss them into the sauce when they're done. Serve them alone or over pasta or rice.

CHICKEN FAJITA CASSEROLE

Serves 4–6

Have you ever been in a Mexican restaurant when someone has ordered the chicken fajitas? The entire restaurant seems to turn their heads when the waiter is walking it to the table. The sizzling on the platter is what gets the crowd's attention, but the smell and the look of the fajitas is what keeps it. Suddenly everyone is wishing they ordered the chicken fajitas. The moral of the story is that everyone loves them. Chicken fajita casserole is so easy to make at home, and you don't even need the sizzling plate. Try these if you need a guaranteed crowd-pleaser at your next family dinner.

2 tbsp (30 ml) olive oil

1 green bell pepper, sliced into thin strips

1 red, yellow or orange bell pepper sliced into thin strips

1 large onion, sliced into thin strips

Salt and pepper, to taste

1 lb (454 g) rotisserie chicken, shredded

1 (1-oz [28-g]) fajita seasoning packet

1 cup (113 g) shredded Cheddar cheese, divided

1 cup (112 g) shredded Monterey Jack cheese, divided

6 oz (170 g) softened cream cheese, cut into cubes

OPTIONAL TOPPINGS

Sour cream

Cilantro

Avocado

Salsa

Tortillas

White rice

Preheat the oven to 375°F (191°C).

In a large pan, heat the olive oil over medium-high heat for about 1 minute. Then add both sliced bell peppers and the sliced onion. Lightly season them with a pinch of salt and pepper. The green and red bell peppers add a nice pop of color to the dish, but feel free to use two of the same if you'd like. They're strictly for looks, not variety of taste. Stir the vegetables once every 30 seconds or so until they're soft. This should take about 5 minutes.

In a large bowl, add the shredded chicken, sautéed vegetables, fajita seasoning packet and half of each the Cheddar and the Monterey Jack. Now add the cubed cream cheese and give everything a nice big stir until it's evenly combined. It's important that the cream cheese is room temperature here. We want to avoid big chucks of cream cheese after it's baked. Everything should be smooth and evenly distributed, so don't skip this step.

Spray a 9 x 13-inch (23 x 33-cm) baking pan with cooking spray and add the chicken fajita mixture. Spread it out evenly and top with the rest of the cheeses. Spray a large piece of tinfoil with cooking spray and place it sprayed side down on top of the casserole. This will stop the cheese from sticking to the tinfoil after we bake it.

Bake for about 20 minutes, or until the cheese is melted. This fajita casserole goes great served over rice. You can always go the traditional route and serve it with tortillas, too. Both are wonderful options!

CLASSIC DINNER COMEBACKS

The classics are making a comeback! Or maybe they never really left in the first place. If that's the case, then you're very lucky. Most people leave their childhood meals in the past. Maybe it's because they feel like they've evolved past them? Whatever the reason, these are the classics done right. The best versions of your favorite old-school meals. Now is the perfect time to rediscover why these recipes became staples in so many homes in the first place. They may have been gone from your recipe rotation temporarily, but they certainly can never be forgotten. Prepare your taste buds for a blast from the past because the classics are coming back.

CHICKEN
CORDON BLEU

Serves 4

Easy, impressive and delicious. These are all of the things that come to mind when I think of Chicken Cordon Bleu. Between the melted cheese, salty ham and breaded chicken, it's clear to see why it became a classic in the first place. This is a meal that the whole family will truly love. It's simple enough to be a great weekday dinner option but looks so fancy that it could easily be served for a special occasion. So whether you're celebrating a special moment or just craving something delicious for dinner, Chicken Cordon Bleu is the perfect choice.

8 thinly sliced chicken breasts

Salt and pepper

1 tbsp (8 g) garlic powder

8 slices Swiss cheese, thinly sliced

8 slices ham, thinly sliced

2 eggs

¼ cup (60 ml) milk

1 cup (108 g) Italian seasoned breadcrumbs

3 tbsp (45 ml) canola oil

4 tbsp (57 g) butter, divided

¼ onion, chopped

4 cloves garlic, chopped

2 sprigs thyme

2 sprigs rosemary

½ cup (120 ml) white wine

1 tbsp (15 ml) Dijon mustard

Fresh parsley, for garnish

Preheat the oven to 350°F (177°C).

First, season both sides of the chicken breast with salt, pepper and garlic powder. Place one slice of Swiss cheese and then one slice of ham on top of each chicken breast. Roll the chicken up and secure it with a toothpick at the seam. Depending on how large the chicken breast is, you may need to add a second toothpick. A good idea is to keep count of how many toothpicks you added. That way you know how many need to be removed when the chicken is done cooking, so none are left behind by accident.

In a shallow bowl, beat together the eggs and milk. In another shallow bowl, add the breadcrumbs. Roll the chicken in the eggs and then roll them in the breadcrumbs. Make sure they're completely breaded all around.

In a large skillet, heat up the canola oil and 3 tablespoons (42 g) of butter over medium-high heat. In batches, add the chicken and cook it until it's golden brown on both sides. This should take about 8 minutes total. Don't worry if it's not cooked all the way through. Remove the chicken, place it into a baking dish and place the baking dish in the oven for 30 minutes, or until the chicken is no longer pink inside.

While that's in the oven, make a sauce in the same pan that we cooked the chicken in. Turn the heat to medium-high again and add the onion. Cook that, stirring every 30 seconds, for about 4 minutes or until the onion starts to soften. Now add the garlic, thyme and rosemary. Cook everything for an additional minute, stirring every 30 seconds or so, making sure the garlic doesn't burn.

Now add the white wine and mustard. Bring it up to a gentle boil, then reduce the heat to low. Cook for another 7 minutes, or until the sauce begins to thicken and reduce. Stir in the reaming 1 tablespoon (14 g) of butter until it's melted.

When the chicken is done, gently remove the toothpicks. Be careful, the chicken will be hot. Pour the white wine sauce on top of the chicken. Garnish with parsley and serve warm.

VLAD'S **VEAL MARENGO**

Serves 6–8

This may only be a classic in my parents' house, but it's still a classic nonetheless. I'm one of four kids and we all have strong personalities. Sometimes our differences make me question how we're even related in the first place. I only mention that because it was a constant struggle for my mom to make us a dinner that we all loved. Her father Vladimir's veal marengo recipe was one dinner that we could all agree on. I considered not including this recipe because it does take a long time to make. But trust me, the end result will be worth every minute of your time. I hope you and your family enjoy it as much as we do. And who knows, it could just become an instant classic in your home, too.

1 cup (240 ml) olive oil

4 lb (1.8 kg) veal shoulder cubes, cut in 1-inch (2.5-cm) cubes

Salt and pepper, to taste

1 cup (120 g) chopped onion

1 cup (101 g) chopped celery

1 clove garlic, crushed

1 cup (240 ml) dry white wine, divided

2 (8-oz [226-g]) cans tomato sauce

2 bay leaves

1 tsp dried oregano

1 tsp dried rosemary

1 tsp dried thyme

1 lb (454 g) mushrooms, sliced

2 tbsp (30 ml) fresh lemon juice

¼ cup (57 g) butter

1 tbsp (8 g) flour

1 lb (454 g) wide egg noodles, cooked

Fresh chopped parsley, for garnish

First heat the oil over medium-high heat in a 6-quart (5.7-L) Dutch oven. Add the veal cubes in batches and cook them until they're browned. This should take about 5 minutes total. Season them with salt and pepper and set them aside.

In the same Dutch oven, add the onion, celery and garlic. Cook, stirring every minute or so, until the veggies are soft. This should take about 5 minutes.

Now stir in ½ cup (120 ml) of the wine, the tomato sauce, bay leaves, oregano, rosemary, thyme, salt and pepper. Add the veal cubes back in and raise the heat to high. Once it starts to boil, reduce the heat to low and simmer it covered for 1½ hours. I know that seems like a long time, but it's important for the veal to become tender. If it looks a little dry or thick while cooking, you can add ½ cup (120 ml) of water.

In the meantime, toss the mushrooms in the lemon juice. In a medium-sized pan over medium-high heat, melt the butter and add the mushrooms. Cook the mushrooms, stirring about every 30 seconds, until they are soft. This should take around 5 minutes.

Now add the remaining ½ cup (120 ml) of the wine and the mushrooms to the veal mixture. Mix the flour into 2 tablespoons (30 ml) of water until it dissolves and add it in too. This will thicken the sauce. Cook this uncovered for another 15 minutes.

Spoon the veal and sauce over the egg noodles. Serve with the chopped parsley as a garnish!

ITALIAN STUFFED PEPPERS

Serves 4

4 green bell peppers, tops cut off and seeds removed

Olive oil

Salt and pepper

½ onion, chopped

5 cloves garlic, chopped

¾ lb (340 g) ground beef

¼ lb (113 g) ground sausage, sweet or spicy

1 tbsp (4 g) Italian seasoning

1 tsp garlic powder

1 cup (186 g) cooked white rice

¼ cup (25 g) grated Parmesan cheese

3 cups (720 ml) tomato sauce

2 cups (224 g) shredded mozzarella cheese

Just the smell of these stuffed peppers reminds me of being at the dinner table when I was a kid. There are many different recipe variations for this dish out there. But this is THE classic one. The original version that you'd expect to be served at grandma's house. Speaking of, my grandmother, Cookie, always served hers in green bell peppers. For whatever reason, everyone seemed to decide that green bell peppers were the only color suitable here. So in keeping with tradition, they're staying.

Preheat the oven to 350°F (177°C).

First, rub the outside of each bell pepper with a little bit of olive oil. Lightly season the outside with a small pinch of salt and pepper. Stand the peppers up in a baking dish. If any of the peppers won't stay up without falling over or seem a little lopsided, don't worry, we can easily fix that. Take a knife and cut off the area that's causing the problem. It will become nice and flat, and the pepper will stand up perfectly.

In a large skillet, heat olive oil over medium-high heat and add the onion. Cook the onion, stirring once every 30 seconds, for about 4 minutes, or until the onion is soft. Now add the garlic and cook it for an additional minute. Stir every 10 seconds or so just to be sure that the garlic doesn't burn. Keep the heat on medium-high and add the ground beef and the sausage. Using a wooden spoon or spatula, break the meat into small pieces while it's browning. Give it a stir every 30 seconds or so until the meat is browned and cooked all the way through. This should take 7 to 8 minutes. Drain any extra fat from the pan and discard it. Now season the meat and onion mixture with salt, pepper, Italian seasoning and garlic powder.

Next turn off the heat and add the white rice, Parmesan cheese and tomato sauce. Give it all a nice big stir and make sure everything is evenly combined. Now using a spoon, evenly divide the mixture into the bell peppers. Top each one with shredded mozzarella cheese. Be sure to shred it yourself, as it will melt way more easily and be creamier than the pre-shredded stuff in a bag that's usually coated with cellulose. This is a common ingredient in pre-shredded cheese known for anti-caking and moisture absorption, which prevents it from melting the normal way.

Spray a large piece of tinfoil with cooking spray and place it sprayed side down on top of the peppers. Doing this will keep the cheese from sticking to the foil when it's removed after baking.

Bake the peppers for 35 to 40 minutes, or until they are tender. The little bit of oil we rubbed on them earlier will help the peppers cook a little faster. We want them cooked but not too soft and falling apart completely. If you like a little more of a crunch to the peppers, reduce the time to about 25 minutes. Let them cool slightly and serve warm.

THREE-CHEESE STUFFED MANICOTTI

Serves 8

Manicotti translates to "little sleeves" in Italian. Little sleeves filled with three different bubbling cheeses smothered in tomato sauce. This is comfort food at its finest. This dish is pretty much a hug on a plate. Maybe that's why they're called manicotti? Because these cheese-filled sleeves are reaching out to you for a culinary embrace. I guess there's a chance I could be wrong about that. But one thing I know for sure is that you'll feel all warm and cozy inside with this on your table for dinner.

4 cups (960 ml) tomato sauce, jarred or homemade, divided

2 cups (492 g) ricotta cheese

2 cups (224 g) shredded mozzarella cheese, divided

½ cup (50 g) grated Parmesan cheese

1 egg

Salt and pepper, to taste

1 tbsp (4 g) Italian seasoning

1 tsp dried oregano

1 tsp garlic powder

1 lb (454 g) manicotti

¼ cup (60 ml) water

Fresh parsley or basil, for garnish

Preheat the oven to 375°F (191°C).

First, add 1 cup (240 ml) of the tomato sauce to the bottom of a 9 x 13-inch (23 x 33-cm) baking dish. To a large bowl, add the ricotta cheese, 1 cup (112 g) of the mozzarella cheese, the Parmesan cheese, egg, salt, pepper, Italian seasoning, oregano and garlic powder. Mix everything together until it's evenly combined.

Next, add the mixture to a large piping bag. If you're like me and don't have a piping bag, no problem. Just use a large resealable plastic bag. Add the mixture and cut a large hole in one of the corners to pipe the filling. It works perfectly!

Now pipe the filling into the dry manicotti shells and place them down into the tomato sauce–lined baking dish. Continue filling the manicotti shells and placing them down into the baking sheet until they're all done.

Now top the manicotti with the remaining 3 cups (720 ml) of the tomato sauce and the water. Adding a little extra liquid here is going to help those manicotti shells cook perfectly.

Then sprinkle the top with the remaining cup (112 g) of the mozzarella cheese. Spray tinfoil with cooking spray and place it sprayed side down onto the baking dish. This step will keep the cheese from sticking to the foil when it's removed later.

Bake for 45 to 50 minutes. This will take a little longer in the oven because we saved a step earlier and didn't boil the shells. In my opinion, this is completely worth the extra time if it means avoiding the hassle of boiling those manicotti shells. Let the manicotti cool slightly. I like to let it sit for 5 to 10 minutes uncovered before serving. I feel that everything holds together much better when it's left to firm up a bit. Sprinkle with some fresh parsley or basil for garnish. A little extra Parmesan cheese here never hurt either. Serve warm.

BETTER THAN
GRANDMA'S
MEATLOAF

Serves 6

As far as classics go, meatloaf is right up there on the top of the list. We've all probably eaten our fair share as kids at our grandparents' house, alongside peas and mashed potatoes too, I'm assuming. This isn't your regular old boring meatloaf though. This recipe is even better than the one you had at Grandma's. Just don't tell her that I said that. This one is loaded with flavor from the inside all the way up to the delicious glaze. Not to mention it couldn't be easier to make. This is a classic that's worth revisiting for sure.

2 tbsp (28 g) butter

½ onion, finely chopped

½ red bell pepper, finely chopped

1 rib celery, finely chopped

1 large carrot, grated

4 cloves garlic, chopped

2 lb (907 g) ground beef

1½ cups (162 g) Italian seasoned breadcrumbs

¾ cup (180 ml) milk

Salt and pepper

2 tbsp (30 ml) Worcestershire sauce

¼ cup (60 ml) ketchup

2 eggs

FOR THE GLAZE

¾ cup (180 ml) ketchup

2½ tsp (10 g) brown sugar

1 tsp yellow mustard

Preheat the oven to 350°F (177°C). Line a baking sheet or roasting pan with parchment paper. Just make sure there's enough of a lip on the pan to hold any grease that will come out of the meatloaf while it's cooking.

First, in a large skillet over medium-high heat, melt the butter. Add the onion, bell pepper, celery and carrot. Cook the vegetables for 5 to 7 minutes, or until they are soft, stirring ever 30 seconds. Then add the garlic and cook everything for an additional minute. Stir every 10 seconds or so to make sure the garlic doesn't burn. Turn the heat off and let the vegetables cool.

In a large bowl, add the beef and breadcrumbs. Pour the milk directly over the breadcrumbs and let them soak it up for 1 to 2 minutes. Doing this is great for two reasons—it keeps the meatloaf from getting too dry, and it also tenderizes the beef. It's a win-win!

Now add the salt, pepper, Worcestershire sauce, ketchup and eggs to the beef and breadcrumbs. Then add the sautéed vegetables and gently mix everything together. Be careful handing the vegetables if they haven't cooled off completely. You want to mix the meatloaf until it's just combined. Do not overdo it on the mixing. Overworked meatloaf will be very dense instead of light and airy like we want it.

Place the beef mixture onto the parchment paper–lined baking sheet. Form it into a meatloaf shape and bake for 30 minutes.

To make the glaze, just place all the ingredients into a small bowl and whisk them together until the brown sugar dissolves. Spread the glaze all over the top of the meatloaf and bake for an additional 25 minutes, or until it's cooked all the way through.

Let the meatloaf rest for about 10 minutes before slicing it. A loose tinfoil tent will help to keep it warm until it's ready to serve.

RESTAURANT-STYLE **EGGPLANT PARMESAN**

Serves 6

Have you ever tried to make eggplant Parmesan at home? Sometimes it's just not the same as when you order it out. Super frustrating, believe me I know. But that's why I named this one "Restaurant-Style" Eggplant Parmesan. I'm going to share all my little secrets to making the perfect eggplant Parmesan at home. Just a couple small changes can really upgrade this dish completely. Thanks to this recipe, you'll never have to go out for eggplant parm again.

2 large eggplants, peeled and cut into ½-inch (1.3-cm) rounds

Salt, divided

½ cup (63 g) flour

Pepper

4 eggs

¼ cup (60 ml) milk

4 cups (432 g) Italian seasoned breadcrumbs

2 cups (480 ml) canola oil

1 cup (240 ml) tomato sauce, jarred or homemade

½ cup (50 g) Parmesan cheese

1 lb (454 g) fresh mozzarella cheese, sliced

Fresh basil, shredded, for garnish

Preheat the oven to 350°F (177°C).

First, lay the eggplant rounds out onto baking sheets and sprinkle them with salt. Let them sit like that for 1 hour. The eggplant will start to "sweat" and bead with water. Doing this will remove all the bitterness from the eggplant. Then rinse the eggplant rounds under cold water and dry them well with a paper towel.

In a shallow bowl, add the flour and season it with salt and pepper. In a separate shallow bowl, beat together the eggs and milk. In a third shallow bowl, add the breadcrumbs. Dip each slice of eggplant into the flour first, then into the egg mixture and lastly into the breadcrumbs. Make sure each piece is evenly coated in breadcrumbs. Continue breading the eggplant rounds until they are all done.

In a large skillet, heat the oil over medium-high heat. Wait until the oil is hot enough, around 350°F (177°C). If you don't have a thermometer, place a wooden spoon into the oil with the handle side down. If little bubbles begin to form around the spoon, the oil is hot and ready for frying. Adding the eggplant too early will make it soggy, so it's important to make sure the oil is ready. Add the eggplant rounds and fry them in batches until they're golden brown on both sides. This should take about 6 minutes total. Once it's done, drain the eggplant on a wire rack and lightly season it with salt.

Lay the eggplant back onto the baking sheets in single layers. Spoon 1 to 2 tablespoons (15 to 30 ml) of tomato sauce onto each one and spread it evenly on top using a spoon. Evenly distribute the Parmesan cheese onto the sauce. Then add a slice of the fresh mozzarella cheese over each eggplant round on top of the sauce and Parmesan cheese.

Place the eggplants in the oven and bake them for about 30 minutes, or until the cheese is melted and bubbly. Serve this hot with shredded basil as a garnish.

30-MINUTE
CHICKEN MILANESE

Serves 4

1½ lb (680 g) thin chicken breast

Salt and pepper

1 tbsp (8 g) garlic powder

¼ cup (60 ml) milk

3 eggs

1½ cups (162 g) Italian seasoned breadcrumbs

½ cup (120 ml) canola oil

2½ cups (50 g) arugula

½ red onion, thinly sliced

½ cup (75 g) cherry tomatoes, halved

¾ cup (84 g) small fresh mozzarella balls, cut into 4 pieces each

Aged balsamic, for drizzling

The only thing better than a light arugula salad sitting on top of thinly sliced chicken cutlets fried to perfection is having it all ready to eat in 30 minutes. This is a dinner that is truly the best of both worlds. The arugula salad is cool and refreshing and complements the crispy warm chicken cutlets perfectly. I make this once a week at my house because I find these flavors absolutely addicting. This is the perfect all-year-round dinner, too. Light enough for the summer, but satisfying enough for those cold winter months. If you've got 30 minutes, you have to try this incredible chicken Milanese recipe.

First, season both sides of the chicken breast with salt, pepper and garlic powder. I get my chicken breasts already sliced thin and prepackaged at the grocery store. If you can't find them for whatever reason, that's no problem. Just slice them thin yourself at home.

In one shallow bowl, beat the milk and eggs together. In another shallow bowl, add the breadcrumbs. Now take the chicken slices and dip them in the egg mixture. Let the extra run off and then dip them in the breadcrumbs. Press down with your fingers to make sure the breadcrumbs are evenly coated onto the chicken.

Once all the chicken is breaded, heat the oil in a large skillet over medium-high heat. Okay, now to get the perfect crispy cutlets we have to make sure that the oil is hot. There's a little test we can do using a wooden spoon. Place the end of the handle into the oil. If little bubbles start to form around the handle, that means the oil is ready to go!

Gently place the chicken into the oil. Once the edges start to brown, that's a great indication that they're ready to be flipped. Be sure not to overcrowd the pan and fry them in batches. Since they're thin, they will be cooked all the way through once they're golden brown. Remove them from the oil and place them on either a wire rack or paper towels to drain. Once all the cutlets are done, set them aside.

In a large bowl, add the arugula, red onion, tomatoes and mozzarella. Season with a pinch of salt and pepper and toss it all to combine.

Now place each chicken cutlet onto a plate and top it with the arugula salad. Evenly distribute the salad between each of the chicken cutlets. Drizzle with however much aged balsamic you'd like!

GNOCCHI
BOLOGNESE

Serves 6–8

Bolognese sauce could be a meal in and of itself if you ask me. It's loaded with vegetables and seasoned beef. Kind of like the Italian version of chili. Most people like to serve Bolognese sauce over a long thick noodle like pappardelle. There's nothing at all wrong with that. It's delicious! But I urge you to try it served over gnocchi. There's something about the hearty sauce that complements the potatoes in the gnocchi beautifully. Beef and potatoes are a classic combo for a reason. They just work so well together. This is one dish that will fill you up and keep you satisfied long after dinner is done.

2 tbsp (30 ml) olive oil

2 large carrots, grated

2 ribs celery, minced

1 onion, minced

1½ lb (680 g) ground beef

2 tbsp (36 g) salt for cooking the gnocchi, plus more for the sauce, to taste

Black pepper, to taste

1 tsp garlic powder

2 tbsp (8 g) Italian seasoning

3½ cups (840 ml) tomato sauce, store bought or homemade

1 lb (454 g) gnocchi

¼ cup (25 g) grated Parmesan cheese

In a large saucepan, heat the olive oil over medium-high heat. Then add the carrots, celery and onion. Stirring about every 30 seconds, cook until the vegetables are soft. This should take about 5 minutes. Don't rush this step—the carrots especially should be soft. They're small enough from being grated that they should cook at the same speed as everything else.

Next add the ground beef and cook until it's browned all the way through. This should take 8 to 10 minutes. As the meat browns, stir it once every minute or so, breaking up the beef into small pieces using your wooden spoon as you go. Drain the pot of any grease and place it back onto the burner over medium-high heat.

Season the beef and vegetables with the salt to taste, pepper, garlic powder and Italian seasoning. Add in the tomato sauce and stir everything together until it's well combined. Once the sauce starts to form little bubbles, reduce the heat to low and simmer it for 20 minutes, stirring once every 5 minutes or so.

While the sauce is simmering, add 2 tablespoons (36 g) of salt to a medium-sized pot of water and bring it to a boil. Adding salt to the water is a great way to season the gnocchi themselves since they will absorb some while they're cooking. Drop the gnocchi into the boiling salted water and cook them according to the directions on the package. But WAIT! Don't drain that pasta water too soon. Just before your gnocchi is ready, take a ladle of that pasta water and add it to the Bolognese sauce. This will help thicken the sauce and give it a little extra flavor, too!

Add the cooked gnocchi to the Bolognese sauce and lightly toss it to combine. Add the Parmesan cheese and then give everything one final toss together. Serve warm with additional Parmesan cheese if you want— which I can't imagine anyone would not want!

TUNA NOODLE CASSEROLE

Serves 6–8

I feel like everyone has a couple of cans of tuna fish in their pantry at all times. And why wouldn't they? They're convenient, delicious and affordable. But how many tuna fish sandwiches can you make? Not that I have anything against them. I love them actually, but sometimes I want something with a little more substance, something hearty and warm that will really fill me up. This Tuna Noodle Casserole couldn't be more perfect to make in this scenario. It's all of those things plus it's not that much more of an effort than making a plain tuna fish sandwich. So next time you're in the mood for tuna, give this recipe a try. Just like I know you've got some cans in your pantry, I also know you're going to love this!

4 cups (640 g) egg noodles

1 (10.5-oz [298-g]) can cream of mushroom soup

1 (10.5-oz [298-g]) can cream of celery soup

1 cup (240 ml) milk

2 cups (268 g) frozen peas and carrots

2 (10-oz [283-g]) cans tuna, drained

½ cup (57 g) shredded Cheddar cheese

Salt and pepper, to taste

½ tsp onion powder

1 tsp garlic powder

4 tbsp (57 g) butter

¼ cup (27 g) Italian seasoned breadcrumbs

Preheat the oven to 375°F (191°C).

Make the egg noodles according to the directions on the package. When they're done, add them to a large bowl along with the cream of mushroom soup, cream of celery soup, milk, peas and carrots, tuna and shredded cheese. Add the salt, pepper, onion powder and garlic powder. Add as much salt as you'd like, but just be aware that the soups and cheese are pretty salty on their own.

Now add the mixture to a 9 x 13-inch (23 x 33-cm) baking dish and spread it out evenly. Bake the casserole uncovered for 30 minutes.

In a small bowl, melt the butter in the microwave for 20 to 30 seconds and add the breadcrumbs. Toss them together and then sprinkle the mixture on top of the casserole.

Turn the oven temperature up to 400°F (204°C) and bake for an additional 10 minutes or until the breadcrumbs are golden and toasted. Serve warm.

CHICKEN
CACCIATORE

Serves 6

Whenever I mention chicken cacciatore, someone always says, "I haven't had that dish in forever," followed by their expression of love for it. I'm not sure why more people don't make this recipe anymore. It's kind of just faded out in popularity over the years, I guess, and for no good reason either. It's super easy to make and absolutely delicious, too. It's about time this dish makes the comeback it deserves. I think maybe people need a reminder of why this became a classic in the first place. Put the once very popular chicken cacciatore on your dinner menu for this week and remember what all the fuss was once about. You won't be disappointed.

2 lb (907 g) boneless skinless chicken breasts

Salt and pepper

2 tbsp (16 g) garlic powder, divided

3 tbsp (45 ml) olive oil

1 onion, cut into thin long slices

1 green bell pepper, cut into thin long slices

4 cloves garlic, minced

¾ cup (180 ml) chicken broth

1 (28-oz [794-g]) can crushed tomatoes

2 tbsp (8 g) Italian seasoning

Pasta or white rice, for serving

First, season the chicken breasts on both sides with salt, pepper and 1 tablespoon (8 g) of garlic powder. In a medium-sized pot, heat the olive oil over medium-high heat. Add the chicken breasts and cook them in batches for about 4 minutes on each side. Remove them from the pot and set them aside once they're nice and browned. Don't worry if they're not cooked all the way through. We'll finish cooking them in the sauce later.

In the same pot, reduce the heat to medium and add the onion and pepper. Cook them for 5 minutes, stirring every 30 seconds or so. Then add the garlic and cook for another minute. This time, stir about every 10 seconds to make sure the garlic doesn't burn.

Now add the chicken broth, crushed tomatoes, Italian seasoning, the remaining tablespoon of garlic powder, salt and pepper. Raise the heat to medium-high and stir every 30 seconds until the sauce starts to boil and little bubbles form. Then reduce the heat to low and let it simmer for 10 minutes, stirring every 2 minutes.

Then add all the chicken back into the pot. Wiggle it down into the sauce to make sure as much of the chicken is covered with sauce as possible. Cover the pot and cook over low heat for about 20 minutes, or until the chicken is cooked all the way through.

Once the chicken is done, turn off the heat and serve it with your choice of either pasta or white rice. Just place a big serving spoonful or two on top of either one!

"SEA"ING IS BELIEVING

I always find it interesting when people tell me that they don't cook fish at home. Oftentimes it's because they consider it intimidating or a difficult food to "get right." I get that. Fish can be a little tricky if you've never cooked with it before. There's a lot to consider like overcooking, undercooking and seasoning choices. I want to show you that it doesn't always have to be a stressful experience. There are plenty of foolproof fish recipes that aren't complicated to make at all. I happen to have a few fantastic ones that I think you'll really love. There's no good reason to cut fish out of your home-cooked meal options. Don't just take my word for it. Try them out for yourself and once you see it, you'll believe it, too.

SALMON CAKES
WITH SPICY SRIRACHA TARTAR SAUCE

Serves 6–8

When it comes to fish dishes, salmon cakes are right up there on my list of top favorites. They're super easy to make and taste absolutely incredible. Serve these with spicy tartar sauce for some kick, and I'm completely sold. I love eating these for dinner, but they can easily be made into smaller portions and served as an appetizer, too, or even alongside a nice juicy steak for a fun spin on traditional surf and turf. There's so much to love about these versatile salmon cakes. Make them and try all the delicious ways they can be enjoyed!

FOR THE SALMON CAKES

1 lb (454 g) salmon filets

4 tbsp (60 ml) olive oil, divided

Salt and pepper, divided

1 tbsp (8 g) garlic powder

1 onion, chopped

½ red bell pepper, diced

1 tbsp (8 g) capers, drained

1 cup (56 g) panko breadcrumbs

2 eggs

3 tbsp (45 ml) mayonnaise

2 tbsp (30 ml) Worcestershire sauce

¼ cup (15 g) fresh parsley, minced

3 tbsp (42 g) butter

Lemon wedges, for garnish (optional)

FOR THE SRIRACHA TARTAR SAUCE

½ cup (120 ml) mayonnaise

½ lemon, juiced

2 tbsp (30 g) dill pickle relish

2 tbsp (30 ml) sriracha

Salt, to taste

Preheat the oven to 400°F (204°C).

Place the salmon skin side down on a parchment paper–lined baking sheet. Spread 2 tablespoons (30 ml) of the olive oil over the filet and season it with the salt, pepper and garlic powder. Bake it for 20 minutes, or until the salmon is cooked all the way through. Set it aside to cool when it's done.

In a medium sized skillet, heat the remaining 2 tablespoons (30 ml) of olive oil over medium-high heat. Add the onion, bell pepper and capers. Cook them for about 8 minutes, stirring every 30 seconds, or until the vegetables soften. Let them cool slightly.

Now, using two forks, flake the salmon into a large bowl, leaving the skin behind on the baking sheet. Add the sautéed veggies, breadcrumbs, eggs, mayonnaise, Worcestershire sauce, salt, pepper and parsley. Stir everything together until is evenly combined and place it covered in the fridge for 30 minutes. This will help the salmon cakes hold together.

While that's in the fridge, make the sriracha sauce by stirring all the ingredients together in a small bowl. Cover it and place it in the fridge until it's ready to be used.

Take the salmon mixture out of the fridge and form it into patties. About 3 inches (7 cm) wide and ½ inch (1.3 cm) thick is a great size. They're easy to handle without flaking apart and they cook through nicely if you stay close to that measurement.

In a large pan, heat the butter over medium-high heat and add the salmon cakes. Fry them for 4 minutes on each side, or until they're golden brown. Drain them on a paper towel when they're done frying. Serve them warm with the sriracha tartar sauce and lemon wedges on the side.

SHRIMP SCAMPI OVER ANGEL HAIR

Most people who like seafood find shrimp scampi completely irresistible. Imagine garlicky, buttery shrimp covered in a white wine sauce. How could you not love that? Serve it over angel hair to soak up every drop of that incredible sauce, and you've got yourself a mouthwatering dinner. Did I mention it's fast and easy to make, too? Winner, winner, shrimp scampi dinner!

Serves 6

2 tbsp (36 g) salt, plus more for seasoning

1 lb (454 g) angel hair pasta

2 tbsp (30 ml) olive oil

4 tbsp (57 g) butter, divided

1 medium onion, chopped

5 cloves garlic, minced

1 lb (454 g) deveined medium-sized shrimp

Black pepper

1 tsp garlic powder

½ cup (120 ml) white wine

¼ cup (60 ml) vegetable broth

1 lemon, juiced

¼ cup (15 g) fresh parsley, chopped

In a large pot, boil water with the salt and drop in the pasta. Cook it according to the directions on the package to al dente. The pasta will boil and absorb some of that salt, giving it a really nice flavor all on its own.

Next, in a large skillet over medium-high heat, melt the olive oil and 2 tablespoons (28 g) of butter. Add the onion and garlic and cook, stirring every 30 seconds or so for about 5 minutes, or until the onion is soft.

Now add the shrimp into the skillet and season them with the salt, pepper and garlic powder. Stir the shrimp about every 30 seconds and cook them for about 3 minutes, or until they turn pink and start to curl slightly. Shrimp cook up fast, so make sure to keep an eye on them. If they curl up too much, that means they're overdone.

Remove the shrimp and place them in a bowl with some tinfoil on top to keep them warm.

Next add the white wine, vegetable broth and lemon juice to the skillet. Keep the heat at medium-high and bring the liquid to a boil. Scrape the bottom of the pan with your wooden spoon to release all the browned pieces. Let this boil for about 5 minutes and then add the remaining 2 tablespoons (28 g) of butter. This will help reduce and thicken the sauce. Be sure to taste it and re-season with salt and pepper if you think it needs it.

Finally, shut off the heat and add the pasta and shrimp back into the wine sauce. Give everything a good stir until it's evenly combined. Sprinkle with parsley.

CREAMY LEMON AND HERB
SALMON PASTA

Serves 8

Fish dishes are generally considered light compared to other protein options. This is very true considering they're usually served alongside vegetables or with a salad. As much as I enjoy eating them that way, sometimes I'm craving something with just a little more substance. This is where creamy lemon and herb salmon pasta fits in perfectly. It's all the delicious flavors of the salmon that I love with the carbs that I want too. The flavors of the herbs and creaminess of the sauce blend the salmon and pasta together seamlessly. It's a great dinner to make when you're in the mood for a super filling salmon dinner.

1 lb (454 g) salmon filets

2 tbsp (36 g) salt for cooking the linguine, plus more for the salmon

Black pepper, divided

4 tbsp (57 g) butter

½ onion, diced small

5 cloves garlic, minced

½ cup (120 ml) white wine

2 cups (480 ml) heavy cream

1 tbsp (6 g) lemon zest

1 tsp garlic powder

¼ cup (25 g) Parmesan cheese, plus more to taste

1 (1-lb [454-g]) box linguine

10 oz (283 g) fresh spinach

4 tbsp (32 g) capers

1 tbsp (4 g) fresh parsley, chopped, plus more to taste

Set the oven to 400°F (204°C). Place the salmon skin side down onto a baking sheet and sprinkle with salt and pepper. Bake for 14 minutes, or until the salmon is cooked all the way through. Set it off to the side and place some tinfoil on top to keep it warm.

In a large skillet with a tall rim, heat the butter over medium-high heat. Please keep in mind that a pound of pasta as well as other ingredients will need to fit inside of it. If your skillet is too small, you can do this in a large pot. Once the butter is melted, add the onion and cook for 4 minutes, stirring every 30 seconds or so. Then add the garlic and cook for another minute, stirring about every 10 seconds so the garlic doesn't burn.

Now add the wine and turn the heat up to high. Cook the wine for 2 minutes, then slowly add the cream, lemon zest, salt, pepper, garlic powder and Parmesan cheese. By heating the wine first, you will cook out some of that harsh alcohol taste. And adding the cream slowly will ensure it doesn't curdle or separate, which will keep the sauce nice and smooth. Once the sauce is boiling, reduce the heat to medium and continue cooking for 5 to 6 minutes, stirring every 30 seconds. Then turn the heat down to low and let it simmer.

Next add the linguine to boiling water with 2 tablespoons (36 g) of salt. Cook the pasta according to the directions on the back of the package. Because you are adding salt to the water, the linguine absorbs some while it cooks. This is the only opportunity to really season the pasta itself.

Keeping the heat on low, add the cooked linguine and spinach to the cream sauce. Gently stir everything together until the spinach has wilted and the linguine is completely coated in the sauce. Add the capers and parsley and give everything one more big stir.

Plate individual servings of the pasta. Then distribute chunks of the salmon on top of each serving of pasta. Because we didn't spray the baking sheet, the salmon should lift easily leaving the skin behind. Garnish with additional Parmesan cheese or parsley if you'd like!

LUMP CRAB CAKE BURGERS WITH TARTAR SAUCE

Serves 4

Crab cakes are my weakness. I love to order them when I'm out to eat. I get them every time that I see them on a menu. Crab meat is so delicate and flavorful. It blends in perfectly with the breadcrumbs and other ingredients to make the most delicious little cakes. I thought I'd had just about every version of crab cakes out there, until one day I saw a crab cake burger on a restaurant menu, and it changed the game forever. I couldn't get over how delicious they were. Now I don't even wait until I'm out to eat. I make them right in the comfort of my own home whenever I want. Which is pretty often. If you're a crab cake fan, I hope when you give this a try, it further deepens your love for crab cakes.

FOR THE CRAB CAKES

1 tbsp (15 ml) canola oil

½ red bell pepper, diced small

½ onion, diced small

Salt and pepper, to taste

1 lb (454 g) lump crab meat

½ cup (54 g) Italian seasoned breadcrumbs

½ cup (120 ml) mayonnaise

1 large egg

2 tbsp (30 ml) Worcestershire sauce

2 tbsp (28 g) butter

1 tbsp (15 ml) olive oil

4 brioche burger buns

FOR THE TARTAR SAUCE

½ cup (120 ml) mayonnaise

½ lemon, juiced

2 tbsp (30 g) dill pickle relish

Salt and pepper, to taste

OPTIONAL TOPPINGS

Lettuce

Tomato

Red onion

For the crab cakes, in a small skillet, heat the canola oil over medium-high heat. Add the bell pepper and onion and lightly season with a small pinch of salt and pepper. Cook the vegetables for about 5 minutes, or until they are soft, stirring about every 30 seconds. When they're done, take them off the heat and let them cool.

In a large bowl, add the crab meat, breadcrumbs, mayonnaise, egg, Worcestershire sauce and cooled peppers and onions. Season with salt and pepper.

Form the crab mixture into four equal-sized patties. In a large skillet, heat the butter and olive oil over medium high-heat. Add the crab patties and cook them until they're browned on both sides. This should take 5 to 7 minutes.

To make the tartar sauce, combine all the ingredients in a bowl and mix well.

Next, split each brioche bun and place some tartar sauce on the bottom bun. How much is totally up to you. Then add the crab patty on top of the tartar sauce. Add whatever additional toppings you'd like and close the burger with the top bun. Serve warm.

BAJA
FISH TACOS

Serves 4

Take the idea of what to expect from traditional tacos and toss it out the window with this recipe. These cod fish tacos are nothing like the beef and cheese version you're used to. They're totally unique in taste, appearance and preparation. They also happen to be out-of-this-world delicious. Keep a mental note of this recipe if you celebrate taco Tuesday. It's a great way to add something different to your usual weekday routine. You absolutely don't have to wait for a Tuesday to make these though. They're just as fabulous any day of the week.

3 tbsp (45 ml) olive oil

1 lime, juiced

1 tsp chili powder

1 tsp paprika

½ tsp cumin

½ tsp cayenne pepper

Salt, to taste

1½ lb (680 g) cod fish, cut into 4 equal-sized pieces

1 tbsp (15 ml) vegetable oil

8 corn tortillas

Sour cream

Salsa

FOR THE CABBAGE SLAW

¼ cup (60 ml) mayonnaise

1 lime, juiced

2 tbsp (8 g) fresh cilantro, chopped

2 cups (240 g) coleslaw mix

1 jalapeño, minced

½ red onion, sliced thin

Salt and pepper, to taste

In a medium-sized shallow bowl, add the olive oil, lime juice, chili powder, paprika, cumin, cayenne pepper and salt. Whisk it together and add the cod filets. Gently coat them in the marinade and place them covered in the fridge for 30 minutes.

While the fish is marinating, make the cabbage slaw. Add all the cabbage slaw ingredients to a medium-sized bowl and toss everything together until it's evenly combined.

Now heat the vegetable oil over medium-high heat and add the cod fish. Cook it for about 5 minutes on each side, or until it's cooked all the way through. Remove it from the pan and let the fish cool slightly. Then gently push down on the fish with a fork and break it into chunky pieces.

Place some of the fish into the center of each tortilla and cover it with as much of the cabbage slaw as you'd like. Drizzle the top with some sour cream and salsa and serve warm.

MUSSELS MARINARA OVER LINGUINE

Serves 6

I can eat more mussels marinara than I'd like to admit. Seriously, those things are so tiny that I feel like I can just eat and eat and eat and never get full. I love them so much though. I don't mind consuming massive amounts for taste over substance. I'll usually make these as an appetizer to something a little more filling. Unless, of course, I decide to make Mussels Marinara over Linguine. Then I can make an entire meal out of it, no problem. The mussels give the marinara sauce such a great flavor, and it's perfect with the pasta. I hope the mussel lovers give this one a try and finally make a whole meal out of these delicious little shellfish.

1 tbsp (15 ml) olive oil

1 onion, diced

4 cloves garlic, chopped

½ tsp crushed red pepper flakes

½ cup (120 ml) white wine

3 cups (720 ml) marinara sauce

1 lb (454 g) mussels, shells scrubbed clean

½ (1-lb [454-g]) box linguine, cooked

Fresh basil, shredded, for garnish

In a large saucepan, heat the oil over medium-high heat. Add the onion and cook it for 4 minutes, stirring about every 30 seconds until the onion begins to soften. Then add the garlic and red pepper flakes. Cook that together for another minute. Stir every 10 seconds so the garlic doesn't burn.

Add in the wine and cook that for 2 minutes to remove the harsh alcohol taste. Then pour in the marinara sauce and turn the heat up to high. Once it starts to bubble, add the mussels and reduce the heat to low. Cover the pot with the lid and cook the mussels for 5 minutes, or until all the mussel shells open. Throw out any shells that don't open up—they are dead and should not be eaten.

Serve the mussels and sauce over cooked linguine. Garnish with shredded basil and serve hot.

FILET OF FISH
SANDWICH

Serves 4

I'm a sucker for a fish sandwich. Some people go to fast-food places for the burgers. Not me; it's the fish sandwiches all the way! I feel like the only people that knock them are the ones who have never had one. Maybe it's because ordering fish from a fast-food place is a turnoff? Okay fine, I get that, but change it. Let's do a homemade fish sandwich, and just try to tell me it's not absolutely incredible. I don't think that's possible. This recipe is even better than any drive-thru version out there. Bold statement, I know, but I'm sticking to it. Whether or not you're an established fish sandwich fan, I wholeheartedly believe this recipe is one that everyone will love.

1 cup (108 g) plain breadcrumbs

2 eggs

2 tbsp (30 ml) water

4 (3-4-oz [85-113-g]) pieces cod fish filet

Salt and pepper

4 tbsp (60 ml) canola oil

4 brioche buns

4 slices American cheese

FOR THE TARTAR SAUCE

½ cup (120 ml) mayo

2 tbsp (30 g) dill pickle relish

½ lemon, juiced

¼ tsp sugar

Black pepper

Place the breadcrumbs in one shallow bowl. In a separate shallow bowl, add the eggs and water and whisk them together with a fork.

Now lightly season both sides of the cod filets with a little pinch of salt and pepper. Dip the fish in the egg mixture and make sure to let the extra run off. We're using this as a binder for the breadcrumbs only. We don't want to include fried eggs as a part of this sandwich, too. Once the egg wash runs off, dip the fish into the breadcrumbs and coat each piece evenly on both sides. Do this until all of the pieces are done.

Heat the oil in a large skillet over medium-high heat. Once the oil is hot, add the breaded fish. Fry them in batches until they're golden brown on both sides. Feel free to make a couple at a time, just don't overcrowd your pan. It will bring down the temperature of the oil and the fish won't be as crispy. Frying them should take 2 to 3 minutes on each side. Once they're done, transfer them to either a wire rack or a paper towel–lined plate and keep them warm.

A filet of fish is nothing without a good tartar sauce. To make that, combine the mayo, relish, lemon juice and sugar. Season with a pinch of pepper and mix it all together.

Another filet of fish component that just makes this sandwich absolutely incredible is steamed buns. Lightly dampen four paper towels with some water and wrap one around each brioche bun. Place them in the microwave for about 50 seconds, and the buns will be perfectly steamed!

Now we're finally ready to assemble the sandwich. Add one slice of American cheese to the bottom bun, followed by one piece of fried fish, then a nice dollop of tartar sauce—how much is up to you, but the more the merrier if you ask me—and finish it with the top bun. Serve warm.

SHRIMP FRANCESE OVER SPINACH

Serves 4

Have you ever been addicted to a food? Meaning you've tried something and loved it so much that it was all you wanted to eat for an extended period of time. Shrimp Francese is my food addiction. I had it while I was out to eat once, and that's all I needed to get hooked. The restaurant shut down shortly after, but in no way could that minor detail stop me. I experimented at home until I got the recipe perfect. Now I can happily feed my addiction in the privacy of my own home. I know if you try this, you'll just love it too. If you find yourself growing maybe a little too attached, just keep in mind that you are not alone.

4 tbsp (60 ml) olive oil, divided

3 cloves garlic, chopped

1 lb (454 g) spinach, rinsed and dried

Salt and pepper, divided

1 lb (454 g) large shrimp, peeled and deveined

1 tbsp (8 g) garlic powder

3 eggs

½ cup (50 g) Parmesan cheese, grated

¾ cup (94 g) flour

3 tbsp (42 g) butter

½ cup (120 ml) vegetable broth

¼ cup (60 ml) white wine

1 lemon, juiced

Fresh chopped parsley, for garnish

In a large skillet, heat 1 tablespoon (15 ml) of olive oil over medium-high heat and add the chopped garlic. Sauté that for a minute only. We don't want that garlic to burn.

Then add the spinach in batches. It will wilt down fast as it cooks. Keep adding the spinach until it is all cooked down. This should take about 5 minutes. Season the spinach with salt and pepper. Turn the heat off on the pan and drain out any extra liquid. Keep the spinach warm until it's time to use it.

With a sharp knife, butterfly the shrimp by cutting each of them down the back until they open up and appear larger. Add the shrimp to a medium-sized bowl and toss them in the salt, pepper and garlic powder until they're evenly coated.

Then in a shallow bowl, whisk together the eggs and the Parmesan cheese. In another shallow bowl, add the flour. Coat the shrimp in the flour, then dredge it in the egg mixture and coat it in the flour again. Continue until all the shrimp are coated.

In a large skillet over medium-high heat, heat the butter and the remaining 3 tablespoons (45 ml) of olive oil together. And add the shrimp. Cook them in batches until they're golden brown on both sides and just slightly start to curl. This will only take about 1½ minutes on each side. If the shrimp start to curl up too much, that means they're overcooked, so be sure to watch out for that and remove them earlier.

In the same skillet over medium-high heat, add the vegetable broth, wine and lemon juice. Once little bubbles start to form, reduce the heat to medium-low and continue to cook it for 3 minutes. Taste the sauce and then season it with salt and pepper.

Plate the spinach and shrimp, and pour the finished sauce over them both. Garnish with parsley and serve warm.

20-MINUTE
SHRIMP AND VEGETABLE STIR-FRY

Shrimp and vegetable stir-fry is easy, delicious and done in minutes. It's a great dinner to make when you've got a really busy day ahead of you but still want to get something on the table for dinner. Any and all vegetables work in this recipe. So feel free to add what you happen to have lying around if you want. When you need a quick dinner that's hassle free and tastes delicious, shrimp and vegetable stir-fry is the one!

Serves 4

¾ cup (180 ml) vegetable broth

¼ cup (60 ml) orange juice

3 tbsp (45 ml) soy sauce

1 tbsp (8 g) cornstarch

½ tsp sugar

2 tbsp (30 ml) vegetable oil

1 lb (454 g) shrimp, deveined and tails cut off

Black pepper

1 tsp garlic powder

3 cloves garlic, minced

1 (1-lb [454-g]) bag frozen stir-fried vegetables, thawed

4 cups (744 g) cooked white rice

In a small bowl, add the veggie broth, orange juice, soy sauce, cornstarch and sugar. Whisk it all together until the cornstarch dissolves.

In a large skillet with a tall lip, heat the oil over medium-high heat and add the shrimp. Season the shrimp with pepper and garlic powder. Stir the shrimp into the oil and cook it for about 2 minutes. Add the garlic and continue to stir and cook for another minute, or until the shrimp begin to curl and turn pink. Remove the shrimp to a plate and keep them warm with a tinfoil tent.

Add all of the vegetables to the skillet and cook, stirring every 10 seconds until the vegetables are warm. This should take about 3 minutes. Add the sauce into the pan and cook everything together for another 2 minutes. Stir about once every 20 seconds.

Add the shrimp back into the sauce with the frozen veggies and toss everything together one final time. Serve it over the cooked rice.

SIMPLE YET SATISFYING
SOUPS, SALADS AND SANDWICHES

You may envision something small when you think of soups, salads and sandwiches. That's normally the nature of these dishes, sure. But these aren't your average light recipes. Each one is a hearty, hunger-satisfying full meal entirely on its own. They're all packed with a ton of different vegetables and lots of protein. They break the mold of what are considered traditional dinner menu options, opening up a completely new door full of culinary possibilities. Soups, salads and sandwiches may not be quite what you'd traditionally go for when planning your dinner menu for the week. But I can assure you that all of these recipes will change your mind about what's considered "dinner" food and what's not.

CRISPY CHICKEN
CAESAR SALAD
WRAP

Serves 4

Crispy Chicken Caesar Salad Wraps are the recipe hybrid that everyone should try at least once in their lives. Part salad, part sandwich, and both parts are equally as amazing. The crispy chicken complements the cool lettuce very well. The wrap adds just the right amount of substance. All of these components make Crispy Chicken Caesar Salad Wraps the perfect weekday dinner choice.

1 lb (454 g) chicken breast

Salt and pepper

1 tbsp (8 g) garlic powder

2 eggs

¼ cup (60 ml) milk

1 cup (108 g) Italian seasoned breadcrumbs

Canola oil, for frying

2 romaine lettuce hearts

½ cup (56 g) shaved Parmesan

½ cup (120 ml) creamy Caesar salad dressing

4 large tortillas

Start by slicing your chicken breasts into bite-sized cubes and place them in a medium-sized bowl. Add the salt, pepper and garlic powder, then mix until the chicken is evenly coated.

Now get two shallow bowls. Add the eggs and milk to one and whisk them together. To the other, add the breadcrumbs. Dunk the cubed chicken pieces into the egg wash and then into the breadcrumbs, coating them completely. Continue doing this until all of the chicken is breaded and set it aside.

In a large skillet with a tall lip, add the canola oil until it covers about 1 inch (2.5 cm) of the bottom of the pan. Heat the oil over medium-high heat until it's ready for frying. An easy way to test if it's ready is to place the handle side of a wooden spoon into the oil. If little bubbles start to form around it, that means the oil is ready to go! Place the chicken cubes into the oil and fry them for about 3 minutes on each side. Do this in batches depending on your pan size. Just be sure not to overcrowd the pan. It will bring down the temperature of the oil if you overload it, and the chicken will end up soggy. Once the chicken pieces are golden brown on all sides and cooked through, place them on a wire rack or paper towels to drain off the extra oil.

Next, cut off the bottom ends of the romaine lettuce and chop it up into pieces. Place the lettuce into a medium-sized bowl and add the shaved Parmesan. I like to use shaved Parmesan in Caesar salads because the quality and texture does make a difference here. You can get prepackaged shredded Parmesan at most grocery stores or do it yourself with a potato peeler and block of cheese.

Now place the crispy chicken cubes into the salad bowl and add the dressing. If you'd like more or less dressing than the amount I gave, just adjust it to your preference. Gently toss the salad to combine all the ingredients together. Evenly distribute the salad mixture into the center of each tortilla. Spread the salad out into a long rectangular shape that fits the length of the wrap. Then just roll it up and slice down the middle in a diagonal crosscut. Serve immediately.

HONEY MUSTARD
CHICKEN COBB SALAD

Serves 6

The first time that I tried this recipe, I made it four days in a row. When I find a recipe that I really love, I go through a heavy food phase with it. That's exactly what happened here. I had never made a honey mustard marinade from scratch before, and I absolutely fell in love with the flavors. There are so many ingredients in this salad to love, but the honey mustard dressing/marinade is truly something special. I hope you give this one a try and it becomes a healthy food obsession of yours too.

FOR THE HONEY MUSTARD DRESSING

½ cup (120 ml) honey

4 tbsp (60 ml) spicy mustard

6 tbsp (90 ml) Dijon mustard

4 tbsp (60 ml) olive oil

3 tbsp (45 ml) white vinegar

4 tsp (12 g) minced garlic

Salt and pepper, to taste

2 lb (907 g) chicken breasts

2 tbsp (30 ml) canola oil

FOR THE SALAD

4 romaine lettuce heads, chopped

2 eggs, boiled and sliced thin

½ cup (56 g) cooked and crumbled bacon

1 cup (155 g) grape tomatoes, cut in half

1 avocado, sliced

½ red onion, sliced thin

1 cup (150 g) crumbled feta cheese

In a medium-sized bowl, add all of the dressing ingredients and whisk them together. Separate the dressing evenly into two different bowls. Cover one of the bowls and place it into the fridge until you're ready to use it.

The other bowl of dressing is going to be used as the chicken marinade. Slice the chicken breasts into bite-sized pieces and then toss them into the marinade. Cutting the chicken up before marinating as opposed to marinating it whole and then cutting it after it's cooked will ensure that each and every bite will be loaded with flavor. Cover the bowl and let it sit in the fridge for a minimum of 2 hours. Overnight works best in my opinion, but do as long as you can.

When you're ready to eat, take the chicken out of the fridge and drain as much of the marinade from the chicken as you can. In a large skillet, heat the canola oil over medium-high heat and add the chicken. Stir once every 30 seconds until the chicken is browned on all sides and cooked all the way through. This should only take about 5 minutes because the chicken is in small pieces and will cook quickly. Once it's done, remove the chicken and place it on a paper towel to drain any extra oil.

Now it's time to assemble the salad. Place all of the remaining salad ingredients into a large bowl and add the chicken on top. Take the dressing out of the fridge and whisk it together one more time. If it seems a little too thick for your liking, add a tablespoon (15 ml) of water to thin it. Drizzle the dressing on top of the salad and serve it immediately.

CREAMY WHITE
CHICKEN CHILI

Serves 6–8

When I hear the word "chili," beef and red sauce come to mind. White chicken chili is the opposite of what you might traditionally think of. I look at this recipe as a very welcomed change. It's nice to switch things up every once in a while. This chili is packed with hearty ingredients and is perfect for cooler weather. I personally think there's nothing better than a nice big bowl of chili to warm you up when it's cold outside. Next time, instead of the regular old chili that you've made a thousand times, give this white chicken chili a try. I think you'll be very happy with the change in your food routine.

1 lb (454 g) chicken breast, cut into ½-inch (1.3-cm) cubes

Salt and pepper

1 tbsp (8 g) garlic powder

2 tbsp (30 ml) canola oil

1 onion, diced

3 cloves garlic, minced

2 (15-oz [425-g]) cans cannellini beans, rinsed and drained

1 (14.5-oz [411-g]) can chicken broth

½ tsp cumin

½ tsp cayenne pepper

½ tsp chili powder

1 cup (240 ml) sour cream

½ cup (120 ml) heavy cream

4 oz (113 g) cream cheese, room temperature and cubed

OPTIONAL TOPPINGS

Sliced jalapeños

Sliced avocado

Shredded white Cheddar cheese

Tortilla strips

In a medium-sized bowl, toss the cubed chicken with the salt, pepper and garlic powder.

In a large pot, heat the oil over medium-high heat and then add the chicken. Cook that for 3 minutes, stirring about once every 30 seconds. Add the onion and cook for another 4 minutes. Keep stirring every 30 seconds and then add the garlic. Stir every 10 seconds for another minute.

Now add the beans, chicken broth, cumin, cayenne and chili powder. Raise the heat to high until little bubbles start to form. Then reduce the heat to low and let it cook uncovered for 30 minutes. Give everything a nice big stir every 5 minutes.

Next stir in the sour cream, heavy cream and cream cheese. Cook this over low heat for another 5 minutes. Stir it all together again right before serving.

Scoop a big ladle or two into a bowl and top it with some of the suggested toppings or whatever you're into. I personally love cheese and jalapeños. Serve it hot!

GREEK TURKEY BURGER WITH TZATZIKI SAUCE

Serves 4

Greek turkey burgers are a great way to switch up your regular burger routine. There are so many interesting flavors going on in this recipe. I particularly love that the feta is blended right into the burger. Every single bite is guaranteed to have a piece of creamy cheese in it. If creamy is your thing, then don't be shy with the homemade tzatziki sauce either. It goes perfectly with the Greek flavors of the turkey patty. I absolutely love how easy and unique this burger is. I know if you give it a try, you'll love it just as much.

FOR THE TZATZIKI SAUCE

½ cup (67 g) grated cucumber

1 cup (240 ml) Greek yogurt

2 tbsp (30 ml) fresh lemon juice

1 tbsp (15 ml) olive oil

2 cloves garlic, minced

1 tbsp (3 g) fresh dill, finely chopped

Salt

FOR THE BURGERS

1 lb (454 g) lean ground turkey

1 cup (156 g) frozen spinach, thawed and drained well

½ cup (75 g) crumbled feta cheese

1 tsp garlic powder

Salt and pepper, to taste

1 tsp dried oregano

4 brioche buns

OPTIONAL TOPPINGS

Thinly sliced cucumber

Thinly sliced red onion

First make the tzatziki sauce so it has a little time for the flavors to combine together. Wring the grated cucumber out in a dish towel to remove the moisture. Place the cucumber in a small bowl and add the yogurt, lemon juice, olive oil, garlic, dill and salt. Stir everything together and place it in the fridge until you're ready to use it.

For the burgers, in a large bowl, add the ground turkey, spinach, feta cheese, garlic powder, salt, pepper and oregano. Mix it together until it's well combined and form it into four burger patties that are equal in size.

Spray a grill pan with cooking spray and heat it over medium-high heat. Place the turkey burgers down and cook them for about 5 minutes on each side, or until they're completely cooked through.

Now open the brioche buns and place about 1 tablespoon (15 ml) of tzatziki sauce down on the bottom bun. Then add the turkey burger and top it with cucumber and onion, if you like. Serve warm.

BROCCOLI CHEDDAR SOUP
WITH GARLIC BUTTER CROUTONS

Serves 4

When I was a kid, the only way I'd eat broccoli was if it was covered in cheese. Now that I'm an adult, I've grown to love the taste of broccoli on its own. That doesn't mean that I don't jump at the chance to still have that incredible broccoli and cheese combo. Luckily for me, this soup is the perfect way to do that. The cheese isn't too much that it overpowers the broccoli. It's just enough that it complements it perfectly. The homemade garlic butter adults it up even more, too. This is a great way to eat a very grown-up version of an old childhood classic.

FOR THE SOUP

¼ cup (57 g/½ stick) butter

½ onion, chopped

4 cloves garlic, minced

4 tbsp (32 g) flour

2 cups (480 ml) vegetable stock

1 large head broccoli, grated

1 large carrot, grated

Salt and pepper, to taste

½ tsp paprika

½ tsp garlic powder

2 cups (480 ml) heavy cream

2 cups (226 g) Cheddar cheese, grated

FOR THE CROUTONS

3 tbsp (42 g) butter

3 tbsp (45 ml) olive oil

3 tbsp (24 g) garlic powder

Salt and pepper, to taste

1 tbsp (2 g) dried parsley

Half loaf French or Italian bread

Preheat the oven to 350°F (177°C). Line a baking sheet with parchment paper.

In a large pot, melt the butter over medium high-heat. Add the onion and cook for about 4 minutes or until it's soft, stirring every 30 seconds. Then add the garlic and cook for another minute. This time, stir about every 10 seconds so the garlic doesn't burn.

Next add the flour to the pot and whisk it in for 2 minutes. The flour will start to darken in color just a little bit, and that's okay! We just want to be sure to cook out that raw flour taste.

Now add the vegetable stock, broccoli and carrot. Using a grater on the vegetables will ensure they're all uniform in size. The small pieces will help them cook and incorporate nicely into the soup. Season the soup with the salt, pepper, paprika and garlic powder. Raise the heat to high and bring everything to a boil. Then reduce the heat to low and simmer for about 20 minutes, or until the carrots are soft.

This is a good time to make the croutons. In a small bowl, add the butter and place it in the microwave for about 30 seconds, or until it's melted. Add the olive oil, garlic powder, salt, pepper and parsley. Stir it all to combine.

Cube the bread into about 1-inch (2.5-cm) pieces and lay them on the parchment paper–lined baking sheet. Pour the butter mixture on top of the bread and toss it together until the bread is evenly coated.

Bake them in the oven for about 15 minutes or until they're golden brown. Stir them once every 4 minutes to make sure they don't burn. Once they're nice and crispy, remove them from the oven and let them cool until we're ready to use them.

Now back to the soup, the next step is to stir in the cream and grated cheese. Stir it all together and cook the soup for another 5 minutes. Serve with the garlic butter croutons on top!

TACO **SALAD**

Serves 4

When I was in college, I took a road trip home with my friend Krystal. Being a broke college kid at the time, I was thrilled when I found out that her mom had dinner for us, immediately followed by confusion once she told me it was taco salad. I had never heard of that before. I mean, I knew what a taco was, and I was very familiar with salads. But I had never heard of them being combined. Well, needless to say I'm still talking about it over 20 years later, so it definitely made an impression. I've had quite a few different taco salads since my trip to Krystal's house. What I've learned is that there are two things that make this particular one a standout: the Doritos® and the Catalina dressing. If you think you've had a good taco salad before and you're missing those two things, then this recipe is going to change your whole perspective on them. You'll be hooked on these just like I became all those years ago.

1 lb (454 g) ground beef

1 (1-oz [28-g]) packet taco seasoning

2 (9-oz [255-g]) bags chopped Romain lettuce

1 cup (172 g) black beans, rinsed

10 cherry tomatoes, halved

½ red onion, sliced thin

¾ cup (85 g) shredded Cheddar cheese

1½ cups (39 g) nacho cheese Doritos, crumbled into bite-sized pieces

1 cup (240 ml) Catalina dressing

OPTIONAL TOPPINGS

Sliced black olives

Sliced avocado

Sour Cream

Salsa

First, cook the ground beef over medium-high heat until it's browned. This should take 5 to 7 minutes. Add the taco seasoning according to the directions on the back of the packet. When the beef is done, place it in a bowl and cover it to keep it warm.

In a large bowl, add the lettuce, beans, tomatoes, onion and cheese. I stopped before the Doritos and dressing because there's one small detail you need to know. They must be added once you're ready to serve the salad. Don't add them before. The Doritos get soggy, so they need to be eaten immediately. So once you're ready to eat, go ahead and add them in.

Add any additional toppings you'd like to the salad and serve immediately.

TRIPLE-DECKER
TURKEY CLUB

Serves 1

There was a pretty solid chunk of time when my brother Keith survived solely off turkey clubs. To say that he had an obsession would be the understatement of the millennium. I'm not going to lie, I judged. With so many options out there, what was the big deal about a turkey club? I just needed to try one for myself and quickly found out. They are incredible! Every sandwich lover's dream. Bacon cooked to perfection, high-quality turkey, three slices of toasted bread, crispy lettuce, ripe tomatoes and mayo. You gotta have the mayo. It all comes together in the most amazing way. Now every time I make one for dinner, I think of how my brother had it right the whole time and how I was so late to the game.

2 tbsp (30 ml) mayonnaise

3 slices toasted white bread

¼ tsp sriracha, optional

3 romaine lettuce leaves, divided

2 slices tomato

4 strips crispy bacon

¼ lb (114 g) deli-style sliced turkey breast

First evenly distribute and spread the mayonnaise over one side of each slice of toast. If you want to spice this sandwich up a little bit, try adding ¼ teaspoon of sriracha hot sauce into the mayonnaise first. It will give it a really nice kick!

Place 1½ lettuce leaves on top of the mayonnaise. Only place it on one of the pieces of bread. Now add the tomato slices and bacon on top.

Next place another slice of toast on top of the bacon, mayonnaise side up. Now add the turkey slices and the rest of the lettuce.

Place the last slice of toast, mayonnaise side down, on top of the lettuce to close the sandwich.

Slice the sandwich in half with a diagonal crosscut. Now cut the halves in half again. You will have four pieces of deliciously tall turkey clubs. I like to secure each piece with a toothpick so I don't have to worry about them flopping to the side and coming undone. Serve immediately!

PASTA
FAGIOLI SOUP

Serves 6

You may have heard this referred to before as "pasta fazool." It's a very commonly used name for this soup. Both names mean the same thing: pasta and beans, which is the main attraction of this delicious recipe. Any soup that's got pasta in it is a win in my opinion. The beans are a very welcome addition also. Between those two things, the vegetables and the delicious broth, pasta fagioli is a favorite among soup lovers. If this happens to be a food you've yet to try, I bet you'll love it just as much as everyone else does. Give it a try and see for yourself.

2 tbsp (30 ml) olive oil

1 onion, diced small

1 carrot, diced small

1 rib celery, diced small

5 cloves garlic, minced

Salt and pepper, to taste

1 (28-oz [794-g]) can crushed tomatoes

2 cups (480 ml) chicken broth

½ lb (227 g) ditalini pasta

1 (15-oz [425-g]) can cannellini beans, drained and rinsed

1 (15-oz [425-g]) can kidney beans, drained and rinsed

2 tbsp (8 g) Italian seasoning

1 tsp garlic powder

Parmesan cheese, for serving

Fresh parsley, for garnish

In a large pot, heat the olive oil over medium-high heat. Add the onion, carrot and celery and cook the vegetables for 5 to 6 minutes. Give them a stir once every 30 seconds or so. Then add the garlic and sprinkle with a pinch of salt and pepper. Cook everything for another minute and stir frequently this time. About once every 10 seconds will keep the garlic from burning.

Now add the crushed tomatoes and chicken broth. Turn up the heat and bring everything to a boil, then add the pasta. Lower the heat to medium-high and let the pasta cook until it's al dente. This should take about 5 minutes.

Next add the cannellini beans, kidney beans, Italian seasoning, garlic powder and salt and pepper to taste. We rinse the beans from the thick goopy liquid they come in to remove the salt and starch before adding them to the soup. This will make sure we get all the great bean flavors with none of that extra stuff. Cook everything for another 3 minutes.

Serve the soup hot in individual bowls. Serve with Parmesan cheese and garnish with a little parsley.

MOM'S
TRICOLORED CHEESE TORTELLINI SALAD

Serves 8–10

Way before the Internet was a thing, my mother found this recipe in a waiting room magazine. Back then, if you saw something you wanted to make, you'd have to quietly rip the page out, careful not to draw too much attention to yourself. Options had to be weighed. Was the risk worth the reward? My mother took a gamble that day, and I'm very pleased to say that it was 100 percent worth it. This tortellini salad recipe is the best! I hope you enjoy this longtime family favorite of ours.

1 lb (454 g) tricolored spiral pasta

1 lb (454 g) cheese tortellini

1 red bell pepper, chopped

1 red onion, chopped

¼ cup (45 g) Kalamata olives, chopped

8 oz (226 g) feta cheese

1 tbsp (5 g) dried oregano

1 (16-oz [473-ml]) bottle of Robusto Italian dressing

First, cook the spiral pasta and the tortellini according to the directions on the back of their packages. After you drain them, rinse them in cold water to stop the cooking process so the pasta holds its shape and doesn't become too mushy.

Put both pastas into a large bowl and add the bell pepper, red onion and olives. Crumble the feta cheese and add it to the mixture. Make sure you get the feta that is in one solid block in a little water, then crumble it yourself. The pre-crumbled feta doesn't taste as good and will not work for this recipe. Sprinkle with the oregano and add the whole bottle of Italian dressing. Stir everything together until it's evenly combined and refrigerate overnight.

Give everything another big stir before serving!

HEARTY
TURKEY STEW

Serves 4

Turkey stew is a special-occasion recipe around here—the occasion being that I actually have leftover turkey. For that reason, I mostly make this only once or twice a year around Thanksgiving. When I do, my family absolutely loves it. Turkey stew is loaded with protein, vegetables and potatoes—everything you need for the perfect hearty meal. You don't have to be like me and wait for Thanksgiving leftovers to make this recipe. It's just as delicious all year round.

4 tbsp (57 g) butter

1 onion, diced

3 carrots, peeled and cut into ½-inch (1.3-cm) pieces

3 ribs celery, cut into ½-inch (1.3-cm) pieces

3 cloves garlic, chopped

1 tsp dried rosemary, plus more to taste

1 tsp dried thyme, plus more to taste

Salt and pepper, to taste

¼ cup (31 g) flour

5 cups (1.2 L) chicken broth

3 cups (440 g) baby potatoes, quartered

3 cups (420 g) cooked and shredded turkey

⅔ cup (160 ml) heavy cream

½ cup (67 g) frozen peas

In a large pot, heat the butter over medium-high heat. Add the onion, carrots and celery. Cook them for 5 minutes stirring once every 30 seconds, then add the garlic. Cook everything for another minute, stirring every 10 seconds or so, making sure not to burn the garlic.

Now add the rosemary, thyme, salt, pepper and flour. Cook this for 1 minute, whisking continuously, then slowly add in the chicken broth. Keep whisking and slowly pouring in the broth. This will keep the base of the stew nice and smooth and avoid chunky pieces of flour.

Next add in the potatoes and season with a little pinch of salt and pepper. Turn up the heat to high until the broth begins to bubble. Reduce the heat to low and cook covered for about 20 minutes, or until the vegetables are soft.

Then add in the shredded turkey and cream. Keep the heat on low and cook uncovered for another 5 minutes. Turn the heat off completely and stir in the frozen peas. Cover the stew and let it sit for 5 minutes to heat the peas through.

Taste the stew before serving and re-season it with some extra rosemary, thyme, salt and pepper, if it needs it. Serve warm!

TASTE OF ITALY
PANINI

Serves 4

The word panini means "small bread" in Italian. Don't let the word small in the title fool you. These pressed sandwiches are loaded with some really big flavor combinations. I was fortunate enough to visit Italy when I was a teenager. Lots of different kinds of paninis were eaten on that trip. Each one was delicious in its own way. The fresh mozzarella, prosciutto and roasted red peppers with pesto is the one that made the heaviest culinary impact on me though. The ingredients were all so simple but came together to create something almost magical. Every time I make one of these at home, I'm temporarily transported back to Italy. I hope when you try this Italian panini you feel a little piece of the country also.

4 ciabatta rolls

½ cup (120 ml) pesto

8 slices mozzarella cheese, divided

16 slices prosciutto

1 (12-oz [340-g]) jar roasted red peppers

2 tbsp (30 ml) olive oil

Preheat your panini press or any double-sided grill to medium-high.

Slice open the rolls horizontally. Spread the pesto evenly on the inside of each sandwich half. Add a slice of mozzarella cheese and 4 slices of prosciutto to four of the sandwich halves. Then add the roasted red peppers. I like to pat them dry on a paper towel to remove just a little bit of moisture before adding them to the sandwich. I think it helps hold everything together once it gets pressed down, but this is totally up to you. Just distribute them evenly and place them on top of the prosciutto. Then finish each sandwich with another slice of mozzarella cheese.

Now brush the outside of the rolls with olive oil and place them into the panini press. Do this in batches depending on how big your press is. Close the lid down until the bread has nice and golden-brown grill marks and the cheese is melted. This should take about 3 to 4 minutes. Make a diagonal crosscut and serve the sandwiches warm.

ACKNOWLEDGMENTS

I'd like to give my sincerest thank you to Page Street Publishing Co., especially to my editor, Marissa Giambelluca, for turning the fantasy of having my very own cookbook into a reality. With most of my recipes being online, this book will be something that I can physically hold in my hands as a proud personal achievement.

I also want to send a big thank you to my management company, The Digital Renegades, to my rockstar mangers, Evan Morgenstein and Christina Brennan, and to everyone who worked beside them to make this cookbook happen. I couldn't have done this without you.

To everyone at Page Street Publishing Co. and The Digital Renegades, I hope you both know how much I appreciate you and this entire opportunity. Thank you so much!

ABOUT THE AUTHOR

TARA IPPOLITO is a self-taught home cook from Bergen County, New Jersey. Better known as "T" across social media, she makes easy-to-follow recipes using familiar ingredients. Tara uses her social media channels to share recipes and cooking tips for everyday meals. Her motivation to share is simple: to inspire people to cook and become more comfortable in their own kitchen.

As a wife and busy mother of two little boys, she's always cooking fast family-friendly meals.

Her recipes and cooking hacks have been mentioned on Food Network, *Good Morning America*, Daily Mail, LADbible and many others. Her recipes have also been seen on the daytime TV show *RightThisMinute*. Tara even gained the attention of Gordon Ramsay with her chicken nugget Parmesan sliders and was honored to be featured in one of his famous #ramsayreacts videos. Tara was a contestant for the show *Unbox'd* on So Yummy. She will also be on a cooking competition show coming out on Netflix in the fall of 2022.

As her social media platforms continue to grow, she is committed to delivering consistently delicious content to anyone and everyone who wants to learn.

INDEX